Raising Unselfish Children *in a* Self-Absorbed World

Jill Rigby

HOWARD BOOKS
A DIVISION OF SIMON & SCHUSTER
New York   London   Toronto   Sydney

Published by Howard Books, a division of Simon & Schuster, Inc.
1230 Avenue of the Americas, New York, NY 10020

HOWARD
BOOKS

Raising Unselfish Children in a Self-Absorbed World © 2008 Jill Rigby

ISBN-13: 978-0-7394-9551-3

Manufactured in the United States of America

Edited by Liz Heany
Cover design by John Lucas
Interior design by Davina Mock-Maniscalco

Scripture quotations not otherwise marked are taken from the *Holy Bible, New International Version*®. Copyright © 1973, 1978, 1984 by International Bible Society. Used by permission of Zondervan. All rights reserved. Scripture quotations marked KJV are taken from the *Holy Bible, Authorized King James Version*. Scripture quotations marked MSG are taken from *The Message*. Copyright © 1993, 1994, 1995, 1996, 2000, 2001, 2002. Used by permission of NavPress Publishing Group. All rights reserved. Scripture quotations marked NLT are taken from the *Holy Bible, New Living Translation*, copyright © 1996. Used by permission of Tyndale House Publishers, Inc., Wheaton, Illinois 60189. All rights reserved. Scripture quotations marked NKJV are taken from the *New King James Version*. Copyright © 1982, 1988 by Thomas Nelson, Inc. All rights reserved.
Note: "Wise Old Wilbur" is the mascot for Manners of the Heart's children's program.

To
parents
courageous enough to
live as givers
for the sake
of their children.

———————

Give and it will be given to you.
A good measure, pressed down,
shaken together and running over,
will be poured in your lap.
For with the measure you use,
It will be measured to you.

Luke 6:38

Contents

v

CONTENTS

PART THREE: REBUILDING OUR WORLD

Acknowledgments

DON'T THINK FOR one minute I wrote this book by myself. Far from it. These folks did a lot more work than I did. My deepest gratitude for those who walked this journey with me . . .

Boyce and Chad, you two are the reasons for this book. You taught me much more than I ever taught you in the twenty-five years since your birth.

Liz Heaney, what would I do without you? You organized my terribly disorganized thoughts. You made sense of my nonsense. You pulled it out of me, one word at a time.

Philis Boultinghouse, your patient persistence was amazing.

John Rosemond, lending your expertise to open this book is greatly appreciated. Your friendship is treasured.

Shawna Gose, you've lived through this process, and much to my amazement, you're still here at my side.

Jane Cooper, you allowed me the freedom to be vulnerable.

Dean Cooper, you inspired me to go deeper in God's Word.

Emily and Ferdinand Cavalier, you are the real parenting experts.

ACKNOWLEDGMENTS

Your seventy-six years of enduring love and humble confidence touched my soul and warmed my heart.

Chrys Howard shared her home with my readers.

Gerrit Dawson shared his wisdom as a father and minister.

Larry and Virginia Simeral shared their knowledge and love of movies with a purpose.

Nancy Sebastian Meyer shared her amazing story of forgiveness.

Jerrie LeDoux shared stories of her precious children.

The Worship Team of First Presbyterian Church in Baton Rouge didn't forget me.

My AWSA sisters prayed and listened and helped.

The team at Howard Books continues to make me a part of the family.

The many neighbors and friends who asked, "How's the book coming?"

And to the One who makes all things possible, I give you all the praise and glory and honor today and everyday. Thank you, Lord, for lessons learned the hard way. They're the ones that enable us to help others.

Foreword

JOHN ROSEMOND

I OFTEN TAKE POLLS in my audiences, one of which begins with me saying, "Raise your hand if you believe it's a good thing for a child to have high self-esteem."

In an audience of 500 people, at least 450 hands go up. Interestingly, the people who have their hands in their laps are generally my age (sixty) or older, folks who grew up before the psychological parenting revolution that swept America in the 1960s and early '70s.

"You've raised your hand because you've heard the high-self-esteem mantra over and over and over again," I then say. "Nearly everywhere one turns in America these days, one hears that high self-esteem is a good thing. But I challenge you to accept that you've never really given this much thought. You've never asked why it's a good thing or how the experts came to the conclusion it's a good thing. So now I'm going to speak to your common sense—I'm going to speak to the truth that the Bible says is written on your heart. Raise your hand if you'd rather have a next-door neighbor who has high self-esteem as opposed to a neighbor who is humble and modest."

No hands go up, so I go on.

"Raise your hand if you'd rather be employed by a person who possesses high self-esteem as opposed to someone who is humble and modest."

No hands, but a smattering of laughter as people begin to realize that the propaganda they've accepted is contradicted by common sense.

"Raise your hand if you'd rather have an employee with high self-esteem as opposed to an employee who is humble and modest."

Again, not a hand goes up.

"And now, the biggie: Raise your hand if you'd rather be married to a person with high self-esteem as opposed to a person who is humble and modest."

And again, no hands, but plenty of laughter as husbands and wives exchange knowing looks.

Jesus says that the opposite of high self-esteem ("Those who exalt themselves") is humility ("will be humbled"), and He makes it as clear as clear can be that high self-esteem, the uplifting of self, is not the ideal. In the Sermon on the Mount, he blesses the meek, the poor in spirit, and those who mourn. The words of our Lord are hardly consistent with the notion that it is functional to think highly of oneself. The overwhelming majority of psychologists, of which I am one, say just the opposite. Who are you going to believe? Psychologists or Jesus?

Even good social science confirms the biblical view. Self-esteem researchers find that the higher one's self-esteem, the lower one's self-control; the higher one's opinion of oneself, the lower one's respect for others. The research even finds, contrary to the propaganda, that high self-esteem results in lower, not higher, achievement. Why? Because people who think highly of themselves believe that anything they do is worthy of merit. They feel entitled to praise; therefore, they don't feel obligated to earn it.

Parents are right, however, to have problems with the currently (but not historically) radical notion that high self-esteem is not the grand thing it has been promoted as being. The concern voiced most often is that a child who lacks high self-esteem will also lack self-confidence. The fact is that when humility and modesty were the ideal, America did not lack for people with self-confidence. By all accounts, both George Washington and Abraham Lincoln were examples of humility and modesty.

When I was a child, parents and teachers did not allow high self-esteem. It was called "acting too big for your britches" or "being up on your high horse." You were told, in no uncertain terms, to either fit yourself to your britches or bring yourself back down to terra firma. No one talks to children like that anymore. Why? Because stern reprimands of that sort might harm self-esteem.

High self-esteem has lowered school achievement. High self-esteem has eroded children's manners. High self-esteem has contributed to children becoming materialistic, selfish, inconsiderate, and disrespectful of adult authority. Ironically, high self-esteem has also contributed to the alarming rise in child and teen depression and suicide rates. Researchers have found that people with high self-esteem don't deal with failure and disappointment well at all.

It seems that any way one looks at it, the conclusion can only be that high self-esteem has not helped America's kids be the best people they are capable of being. It has been a hindrance to achievement, functional social relationships, and good mental health.

It's high time parents and teachers began helping rid America of this infection. Reading Jill Rigby's most excellent book is a great place to get started.

September 19, 2007

Introduction

I BEGAN THE JOURNEY of understanding children twenty-five years ago when my identical twin sons were born. Those five-pound sacks of sugar filled our home and consumed my life in one glorious moment. Before their arrival our house was a comfortable, peaceful place for two adults working together to find their way through school, marriage, and life. After our children's birth our quiet home became a busy nursery. Two swings replaced an overstuffed chair in our tiny living room. Two, yes, two playpens lined the wall opposite the swings. Two high chairs filled the breakfast nook, leaving us just enough room to squeeze past the chairs on our way to the kitchen.

My daily ritual of rising early to see my husband off to work, dress, and then head out to conquer the world of interior design was radically changed. The cost of daycare for two trumped my salary. Our pocketbook and our hearts told us I needed to spend my days at home with our sons, a decision for which I have been forever grateful.

I traded in my business suits for jogging suits and replaced discussions of new sofas and fabrics with talk of potty training methods and changing "poopy" diapers. Despite the new challenges and odors, which could be downright disgusting, I loved being a mom. I found great dignity in changing those diapers. I now had a higher calling to give of myself in raising two little boys who would one day become men who would give of themselves to the world.

I was filled with more questions than I ever had in design school. Who could I turn to with answers to my parenting questions? My own mother, of course. She offered her experiential wisdom and then recommended I use my one-track mind to my advantage.

I set my one-track mind in motion and became focused on parenting. I read everything I could find—from Dr. Spock to Dr. Dobson. From Penelope Leach to Terry Brazelton. I read deep psychological perspectives on the evolution of child-rearing in America and easy-to-read commonsense commentaries about raising "happy" children. If a book was in the parenting section, I pulled it down and devoured it.

What did I learn? Truth be told, after reading what the experts had to say, this first-time mom had more questions than answers. Should I put my babies on scheduled feedings, as my mother and grandmother had done, or should I feed them on demand, per the advice of current experts? One insisted that my sons needed to know the alphabet by the age of two, their addition tables by the age of three, and that they *had to* read by the age of four or they would never succeed in school. Another said that children need free play, and lots of it, to be prepared for socialization in school. It seemed the experts disagreed on every issue but one. There was a consensus that children need to feel good about themselves.

In many ways I bought into this philosophy. That is, I did until my sons entered kindergarten and I began to see the results. My attempts to reason with my five-year-olds created half-hour discussions that left me exhausted and my sons just as confused about what I had asked them to do as they had been thirty minutes earlier. When I allowed my sons to choose their menu for dinner, our mealtimes were often miserable because invariably they chose something we didn't have on hand, became upset, and then refused to eat anything else. I was trying my best to let my children decide what they wanted to do when they wanted to do it, as the experts had instructed, but I was beginning to think that maybe this instruction was nonsense. Then, when I read that I would damage my sons' self-esteem if I didn't applaud them with a "good boy" and a treat every fifteen minutes, I knew that what I'd been reading was ridiculous.

I wanted to raise sons who would become productive members of society, not puppy dogs who only did as they were told in order to receive a treat. I didn't want my children to expect special treatment or to be unable to function without applause. I didn't want them to grow up as greedy little monsters. I wanted to raise gentlemen who could put the needs of others ahead of their own wants. Anyone who's been through the "me, mine, and what's-yours-is-mine phase" of a two-year-old knows that all of us are born selfish. *I didn't want to feed my boys' innate selfishness; I wanted to get rid of it.*

I continued my study, although I narrowed my sources as the years passed. I threw out the philosophies that didn't work and kept only the ones that did. I read Scripture with new eyes, looking for the jewels that spoke directly to shaping and molding my sons to become the men God created them to be. I wanted to do my part without interfering with God's part.

As I've worked with children and parents over the last twenty years, I've become convinced that our overemphasis on self-esteem and happiness is the reason our society has become self-absorbed, self-conceited, and self-consumed.

In the following pages, we'll take a closer look at the evidence, and at how you can reverse this trend and empty your child's heart of self-centeredness and fill it with others-centeredness. I'm not going to give you easy answers. There are none. But contrary to the thinking of today, there *are* incorrect and correct answers. I'll do my best to give you correct answers.

Raising unselfish kids is difficult, but I assure you, it *is* possible, and the results are well worth it.

PART ONE

Reassessing the Goal of Parenting

For Our Children

Father, hear us, we are praying,
Hear the words our hearts our saying,
We are praying for our children.
Keep them from the powers of evil,
From the secret, hidden peril,
From the worldling's hollow gladness,
From the sting of faithless sadness,
Holy Father, save our children.
Through life's troubled waters steer them,
Through life's bitter battle cheer them,
Father, Father, be Thou near them.
Read the language of our longing,
Read the wordless pleadings thronging,
Holy Father, for our children.
And wherever they may bide,
Lead them Home at eventide.

Amy Carmichael[1]

CHAPTER 1

The Mirror or the Window?

*O*NCE UPON A TIME *a queen sat at her spinning wheel, gazing through a nearby window and thinking of her child to come. She imagined a daughter with ebony hair, rosy-red cheeks, and skin white as snow. Sadly, the queen died after giving birth to a precious princess, who possessed all the qualities the queen had hoped for.*

In time, the king took for himself another wife. She was beautiful, but she was also proud and arrogant, dismissive of her new daughter, and unable to bear the thought of anyone surpassing her in beauty.

Every morning the queen stood before her magic mirror and inquired, "Mirror, mirror, on the wall, who in this land is fairest of all?"

To this the mirror answered, "You, my queen, are fairest of all."

The queen was satisfied, for she trusted the mirror spoke the truth.

The sweet princess, who was called Snow White, grew up to become even more beautiful than the queen. One day when the queen queried her mirror. "Mirror, mirror, on the wall, who in this land is fairest of all?" the mirror answered, "You, my queen, are fair; it is true, but Snow White is a thousand times fairer than you."

The queen was outraged; envy and pride grew like a weed in her heart until she had no peace day or night. The vain queen ordered a huntsman to take Snow White into the woods to be killed. But he had kindness and spared her life and warned her that she wouldn't be safe from the wicked queen unless she hid in the woods.

Deep in the woods Snow White found a small cottage that belonged to seven dwarfs, who welcomed her into their lives. She found contentment as a humble servant to her adoring dwarfs, until the wicked queen showed up and fed her the poisonous apple. But not to fear, a handsome prince rescued Snow White and they lived happily ever after. The queen? "She was forced to dance in red-hot shoes till she fell down dead."[2]

I don't believe in fairy tales, but I do believe we can learn a lot about human nature from the retelling of familiar stories of old.

Why couldn't the vain queen be content to be a beautiful woman? What happened in her childhood that made her so desperate to be the most beautiful woman in the world? Why was the mirror her best friend? Why couldn't "enough" be enough?

The selfish queen had no empathy for a poor child who had lost her mother, and her cruelty forced her stepdaughter to flee the home she knew. The queen was so focused on herself that she couldn't see the child who desperately needed a mother's love. Choosing to cling to fleeting satisfaction that was here today and gone tomorrow, the queen denied an innocent child the love she deserved.

Just as the mirror magnified the queen's self-absorption, so it is with us. When we look at the world through a mirror, we view each event, every word and circumstance, as how they affect *us*. Our innate selfishness is magnified, and we give way to the part of our heart that desires to have it "my way," to the place of self-centeredness that wants to be worshiped and adored.

Now we see but a poor reflection as in a mirror;
then we shall see face to face.
Now I know in part; then I shall know fully,
even as I am fully known.

1 CORINTHIANS 13:12

Sad to say, many parents have led their children to the mirror by telling them through words and showing them in actions that "It's all about you." Of course, parents don't intend to send this damaging message, but in their desire to give their children what the experts say kids need—high self-esteem—parents often hand children a mirror as soon as they are born. In their desire to make their kids "happy," many parents smother their children with attention, lavish gifts for every A, and tell them they can be anything they want to be, do anything they want to do, and have anything they want to have. Out of a desire to help their children feel good about themselves, parents often crown their kids as prince or princess of their domain.

But rather than growing up to be grateful, selfless, and thankful, these children are turning out to be ungrateful, greedy, and resentful, even toward their parents—the very folks who have given them everything. And why not? Children who look at the world through a mirror see themselves and no one else—yet they are never satisfied.

The Mirror
One day a rich man of a miserly disposition visited a rabbi,
who took him by the hand and led him to a window.
"Look out there," he said.
The rich man looked out into the street.
"What do you see?" asked the rabbi.
"I see men, and women and little children," he replied.
Again the rabbi grabbed his hand and took him to a mirror.
"What do you see now?"

"I see myself," the rich man replied.
"Behold, in the window there is glass
and the mirror is glass also.
But the glass of the mirror is covered with silver.
No sooner is silver added than you cease to see
others and see only yourself." [3]

But what if we put the mirrors down? What if we helped our children see beyond themselves? What if we led our children to the window? The following story gives us a glimpse of what could happen.

———————

Mary Lennox was a most disagreeable child. A classic aristobrat. And rightly so. Her father was a high-ranking British government official in India. Her self-indulgent mother found little time for her daughter because she was always busy with social functions, beauty treatments, and gazing in her mirror.

No wonder Mary never smiled. She raised herself while servants looked after her needs. She could have anything she desired, with one exception, the attention of her parents. By the time she was ten she was filled with arrogant bitterness, so self-consumed she demanded that others bow to her every whim.

Mary's aunt and uncle, Archibald and Lilias Craven, lived on a beautiful country estate in Yorkshire, England, with their son, Colin. Lilias was a wonderful mother. She lived her days sharing the wonder of God's creation with her husband and son in their garden. Tragically, Lilias passed away when Colin was a young child. In deep grief, Archibald withdrew into himself, closing his heart to Colin and the gate of the garden to all.

When a cholera epidemic in India took the lives of Mary's parents, she was sent to live with her uncle Archibald. There she found her cousin to be as miserable as she was. Ten-year-old Colin had not walked since his mother died. He spent his days in bed, self-absorbed in his fear, convinced he would contract a terrible disease if he dared venture outside his bedroom walls. His father spent his days traveling through Europe to escape his pain. Colin longed for his father's affection. Instead, servants waited on him hand and foot to keep him calm and satisfied.

One foggy morning Mary discovered the overgrown gate and entered the garden. She walked among the out-of-control weeds and forgotten plants. Her heart beat a new rhythm at the thought of bringing the garden back to life for Colin and his father. She longed to give herself in service, so that she might forget her own misery.

With the help of a new friend, Dickon, Mary spent her days pulling weeds and planting new flowers. She poured herself into the garden, finding a new life through giving rather than taking.

Mary shared her newfound exuberance for life with Colin, urging him to look out the window of his bedroom and to venture into the world beyond. She encouraged him to "get over himself" and come help in the garden as a gift for his father and to honor his mother's memory. Mary's love for the garden gave Colin the courage to try.

With Mary and Dickon's encouragement Colin made daily trips to the garden. No longer did his window serve as a reminder of the world that had left him behind; it became a passageway to freedom as light poured in each morning bringing new opportunities.

As days passed, the children's former self-centeredness turned to self-forgetfulness. Achy muscles and hot temperatures didn't deter their work. The misery that had consumed their minds disappeared as their hearts filled with compassion. They stopped dwelling on what they didn't have, because they found what they needed, a purpose beyond themselves, not in serving themselves, but in serving others.

Colin soon found the courage to put his feet on the ground. His legs quivered under the weight of his body as he took his first steps. Just like a newborn lamb who finds his legs, Colin's wobble soon became a steady gait.

Receiving word that his son desperately needed him, Archibald rushed back to the estate to find Colin running to meet him. His son's unselfish love broke through Archibald's self-inflicted prison and set him free.

————————

Francis Hodgson Burnett's timeless characters in *The Secret Garden* lost their self-absorption and became who God created them to be when they looked beyond themselves to discover the love they needed. Mary found purpose in God's creation as she worked tirelessly to restore the garden to its former beauty. Archibald's heart opened to see how much his son needed him. And Colin? He found the courage to become who he was created to be when he "got over himself" and left his sorrows behind for joy in the garden.

In *The Secret Garden*, the children had to find their own way to the windows in their lives. But when parents lead children to see the world through a window rather than in a mirror, they take on the role God intended for them, and they teach their children to focus on how *others* feel and what *others* need.

And the amazing thing is that when children look through the window at the world beyond, their own image is reflected back to them in the glass—but it's in the appropriate context, as part of the world, not the center of the world. When your children look beyond themselves, not only can they see others, they also find their purpose in serving others. They find respect for themselves as children of God, and this enables them to step into the world beyond the window to love others as they have been loved.

If we don't empty our children of their self-centeredness, which is our duty as parents, not only will they be intolerable to live with, they'll never become mature adults. If we don't teach our children to turn their attention away from the mirror and look out the window to the bigger world, sooner or later someone else will shatter their mirror for them—and chances are, it won't be pretty. Evidence of this is rampant today.

PORTRAITS OF CHILDREN WHO LOOK AT THE WORLD THROUGH A MIRROR

Timothy's Troubles

Five-year-old Timothy just won't take no for an answer. Yesterday when he accompanied his mother to the grocery store, he incessantly begged her for a treat. Initially she tried to resist, taking the easy way out, but eventually she gave in and bought her son a lollipop. As they were leaving the store, an elderly woman offered Timothy a fresh cookie from the deli. As he dropped the lollipop, he grabbed the cookie, and then demanded that the woman give him another for his other hand.

"Timothy, say thank you to the nice lady," Mom reminded her son. He shook his head while bellowing for the treat he had dropped. Mom apologized to the woman, but her son didn't, nor did he say thank you.

By the time Timothy and Mom arrived home, the cookies were on the floorboard and the lollipop was stuck to the backseat. Now Timothy was really upset. When his mom tried to console him, he kicked at her and yelled, "Get away."

Too bad Mom was more concerned about Timothy's happiness than about his ability to feel gratitude.

Jenny and the Jealous Girls

Throwing her backpack on the counter, twelve-year-old Jenny complained, "They all hate me. Another slumber party and I wasn't invited. I just don't get it, Mom. What's their problem? I have the coolest clothes. I know all the right things to say. If that's not good enough for them, I don't need 'em to be my friends. I'll find other friends."

"Honey, it's not you . . . they're just jealous. There's nothing you can do to help girls who envy you," Mom replied, consoling her daughter.

9

Trouble is, Jenny finds jealous girls no matter where she goes. A couple of months earlier she had made the same remark to her mother. With Mom's support, Jenny had transferred from one homeroom class to another in order get away from another group of "jealous" girls.

Out of her desire to keep her daughter happy and to feel good about herself, Jenny's mom isn't helping her daughter learn that to have a friend, you must be a friend.

Sarah Has Stars in Her Eyes

Sarah constantly pores over celebrity magazines and never misses the television talent shows. She recently auditioned for her high school play, wanting it to be her turn in the spotlight. But the world came to an abrupt halt for this starry-eyed sixteen-year-old when she was given the supporting role, not the lead. Devastated, she returned home to the comfort of her bedroom and the stuffed animals on her bed. Even though Sarah had just started taking voice and dance lessons, her parents responded to the news by telling her that she had more raw talent than any of the older girls, even though she hadn't studied as long as they had.

The following morning Sarah quit the play, saying that she couldn't settle for second-place billing. She and her parents had decided to look for a school that "would better appreciate" her talent.

Sarah's parents don't understand that they're not helping their daughter, they are instead hurting her by pumping her up with false praise, causing her to have an inflated view of her abilities.

Jonathan's Ladder to Success

Twenty-six-year-old Jonathan moved back home last month. Even though his classmates had voted him as "Most Likely to Succeed" his senior year in high school, Jonathan hasn't lived up to that promise. In college he had trouble making it to class on time because his alarm clock wasn't enough to rouse him. He didn't have a clue how to balance a checkbook, wash clothes, or cook a decent dinner. With no one around to take care of him, he couldn't take care of himself. He changed his major four times before earning a degree in general studies.

Following college, Jonathan didn't fare any better in the job market. When he did land a job, he didn't keep it for long. He always had a reason, of course: unreasonable expectations or hours that were "too regular." The source behind Jonathan's dissatisfaction? He had expected to start at the top without climbing the ladder. After all, hadn't he been guaranteed success?

Jonathan's parents had spent years taking care of their son rather than teaching him how to take care of himself, and now he's back home, totally dependent on them. They aren't happy about it, but don't know what else to do.

Timothy, Sarah, Jenny, and Jonathan were all taught to look at the world through a mirror. Now let me introduce you to some children who have been taught to look at the world through a window.

PORTRAITS OF CHILDREN WHO LOOK AT THE WORLD THROUGH A WINDOW

Jason's Birthday Party

Kids were running around in circles laughing those silly, giggly laughs that only five-year-olds can laugh. Jason's birthday party was going smoothly. No tears, hitting, pushing, or biting. When Jason began unwrapping his presents, Samantha and Julie started arguing over a pink party hat. Julie had a blue hat, but she really wanted Samantha's pink hat. Timothy wanted every toy Jason opened. Even Jason was only interested in finding the coolest of the cool in his gifts. He would open one, say thank you, and then open another, until he opened the dump truck of all dump trucks—bright yellow with shiny wheels. He jumped up from the table to take his new, super-duper dump truck to his room.

Jason forgot about the other kids for a moment. He didn't mean to be unkind. A part of his heart wasn't at the party, but with his best buddy, Tommy, who was home in bed with the flu. Jason was worried about his friend and sad he wasn't there to celebrate with him. When the last guest left, Jason asked his dad if he would take him to visit Tommy. Jason's parents were always talking about how they could help other people, so it's no wonder he had such compassion for his friend. His mom was constantly making casseroles for friends who were sick and his dad cut the grass for their elderly neighbor every week.

Tommy's mom answered the doorbell to find Jason holding a shiny new dump truck. She invited him in and Jason ran to Tommy's room with the dump truck in tow. "Tommy, I brought you the coolest truck I've ever seen. Hope it makes you feel better."

Jason had learned at the tender age of five that it really is better to give than to receive.

Rebekah Doesn't Wanna Be a Wannabe

Rebekah's glad it's almost Christmas vacation. She's ready for a break from her busy schedule—homework, two after-school clubs to keep up with, and piano lessons. She's looking forward to just hanging out with a few friends during the holidays. She's not a part of the "in" group, but that doesn't bother her. She'd rather have a few true-blue friends than be in the popular crowd.

Last year some of the cool girls had befriended Rebekah, and for a semester she had a taste of living the "it" girls' life, with all its back-stabbing, gossip, and boy craziness. She had even turned her back on her old friends. When asked what had happened to those new friends, Rebekah said, "Hey, if being cool means you have to pretend to be somebody you're not, I don't want to be cool. I don't wanna be a wannabe! They're soooo into themselves. I know who my real friends are."

Rebekah doesn't have an identity crisis. Her parents have shown her who she is and who she belongs to. She knows that being in the cool group or not doesn't change who she is, a child of God and her parents' daughter. She doesn't need the cool girls to be somebody special. Rebekah has learned that real friendship happens in the heart, not in the superficial stuff the cool girls crave.

Luke's New Jacket

Luke was asked to serve on his tenth-grade court, which meant he would need a new jacket. He and his mom searched for a sport coat that was anything other than navy blue. Luke wanted something different, but different meant big bucks. His family couldn't afford the three-hundred-dollar houndstooth coat they found at a men's clothier, but Luke had a solution—his mom could make him a jacket. She had made a sport coat for his dad years before.

Mom said she would give it a try, under one condition—that Luke would go to the fabric store with her to select the right fabric. He quickly responded to his mom's request, "Let's go." They found the perfect cloth, lining, and leather buttons, all for under thirty dollars.

Luke's mom spent the next two weeks pinning, fitting, and sewing the jacket. During the final fitting she said, "Luke, I know it wouldn't be cool at your school to wear a homemade jacket. I just want you to know I won't tell anyone. It'll be our secret."

When the pep rally was over, the girls in Luke's class came rushing over to his mom to ask if they could learn to sew. Luke had told everyone his mom made his jacket. He wasn't worried about what the kids would think, he was proud of his custom-tailored jacket and his mom, too.

Luke's humility gave him confidence, didn't it? His mom had helped him understand that the man in the clothes is more important than the clothes on the man. No wonder the girls were so impressed!

Alissa's Success in the Real World

Countless job interviews, follow-up thank-you notes, and returned phone calls helped Alissa land a starting position with a new magazine. She didn't get the job she was hoping for, but at least she got her foot in the door. Two-and-a-half years later she received her second promotion. Her boss couldn't stop singing her praises.

Alissa had wanted to quit more than once, because the hours were long, the pay low, and she didn't feel appreciated or respected. She was the young kid on the block and was treated that way. But remembering all those "lectures" from her dad about earning respect kept her hanging in there. When she was discouraged, she would recall his words, "Folks will respect you if you give your very best. Do the right thing because it's the right thing to do, and sooner or later, good things will come." She decided to swallow her pride and accept that everybody has to start somewhere, and for her that meant starting at the bottom. She listened carefully to instruction and followed her assignments to the letter.

Outside the office Alissa volunteers with a youth program in her neighborhood. She's helping young girls with their middle-school writing assignments. A part of her longs to devote all her time to "her" girls.

No one can know for certain where Alissa will be in the years ahead, but one thing's for sure, she is headed in the right direction, as are Jason, Rebekah, and Luke.

———————

So, parent, let me ask you: *Which will you hold before your children— the mirror or the window?*

Our children's point of view makes all the difference in whether they grow up to become selfless adults who function well in the world because they have self-respect or whether they grow up to become self-absorbed adults who can't function well because they feel entitled.

In case you need a bit more convincing, let's take a closer look at the impact the goal of making children feel good about themselves has had on our society and on our children.

CHAPTER 2

"Enough" Is Never Enough

Jill, NOBODY DOES anything for nothing," a friend said a few years ago, trying to console me as I faced disappointment in the actions of a shrewd businessman. But rather than bringing solace, her words sent a cold chill down my spine, and they still haunt me today—"Nobody does anything for nothing."

Is this really true? Have we become so self-absorbed that we've lost the ability to give without expecting something in return?

I believe the evidence says we have. We have forgotten the joy of giving simply to give. Our good deeds are more about us and less about those we serve. Too often we use our good deeds as a foundation for climbing to the top. We point our finger at others, accusing them of being greedy and materialistic, but when we do, three fingers point back at us.

We say we want to raise unselfish children, but we're selfish ourselves. We rationalize our thoughtless decisions. Make excuses for cruel choices. Blame others while forgiving ourselves. Buy things in order to feel better. We encourage our children to share their toys, but do we share our toys? We often tell our kids, "Enough!" But when was the last time we told ourselves, "Enough is enough"?

Let's admit it, we ourselves have self-absorbed hearts in a self-absorbed world.

WANTING WHAT WE WANT WHEN WE WANT IT

We yearn for newer, bigger, faster. We get it and still want more, because newer, bigger, faster can never fill emptiness. We replace blouses, houses, and spouses with the same regularity.

Not long ago I asked a random sampling of adults, ranging from ages twenty-five to sixty, "Why do you replace your household goods, clothing, or vehicles?" Their answers reflected more than just their opinions; their answers reflect our society's mindset:

- "Last year's style."

- "Last year's color."

- "Last year's model."

- "My tastes changed."

- "Our neighbors bought a new one."

- "My best friend bought a new one."

- "I saw an ad on television or online."

- "Read about it in a magazine."

- "New features were added."

- "Makes a task easier."

Not one person answered, "Because it *needed* replacing."

We are a spoiled, throwaway society. We don't buy out of necessity but out of desire. Trouble is, our desires change with the seasons. We toss out seldom-used goods to purchase more of the same. North Americans generate nearly 230 million tons of garbage every year, up from 88 million tons in 1960. During the past thirty-five years, the amount of waste each person creates each day has almost doubled from 2.7 to 4.4 pounds.[1] I wonder how many things and how many relationships could be repaired rather than replaced? How much of what we buy do we really need?

Some folks say we need nothing more than a roof, clothing, food, and four wheels for transportation. Others say we *need* homes with a bedroom for every child, fashionable clothing, delectable food, and vehicles with a bit more than four wheels. Still others say that beyond this we *need* European antiques and oriental rugs to properly appoint our homes, the trendiest accessories to adorn our bodies, gourmet coffee with cream to satisfy our palate, and OnStar to guide our vehicles. We also *need* five thousand square feet of space for our family of four, designer handbags and computer bags to complete our look, sushi and imported cigars three times a week, the latest games for the DVD player in our luxury SUV, and of course, a full entertainment system in our home theater.

Enough is never enough. We want what we want when we want it, and we want it our way.

Since, then, you have been raised with Christ,
set your hearts on things above,
where Christ is seated on the right hand of God.
Set your minds on things above, not on earthly things.

COLOSSIANS 3:1–2

WANTING OUR OWN WAY

More times than not, we live by the same property rules as a toddler:

1. If I like it, it's mine.

2. If it's in my hand, it's mine.

3. If I can take it from you, it's mine.

4. If I had it a little while ago, it's mine.

5. If it's mine, it must never appear to be yours in any way.

6. If I'm doing or building something, all the pieces are mine.

7. If it looks just like mine, it's mine.

8. If I saw it first, it's mine.

9. If you are playing with something and you put it down, it automatically becomes mine.

10. If it's broken, it's yours.[2]

Most of us are more apt to make choices based on "what's good for me" than on "what's good for you." I saw an example of this last year during the holidays. I'd been shopping at a mall and was just as eager to get home as the next person, but when the light turned yellow two cars ahead of me, I stepped on the brakes. Unfortunately, the driver behind me showed her displeasure by blasting her car horn, just as "Have Yourself a Merry Little Christmas" was playing on my car radio.

I glanced in the rearview mirror and saw an impatient female who was not likely to give me a Christmas present, or at least not one I would welcome. The horn blasts continued one after another. My face heated with humiliation. My mind began racing as I waited anxiously for the light to change. *Well, at least my ears and nose are warming up. Wait a minute. Why am I embarrassed? I've done nothing wrong. I'm sure she's tired; but hey, we're all tired. Must be a teenager in a hurry to meet her boyfriend.*

Even though I pounced on the gas pedal when the light turned green, the driver spun around from behind, pulling to the right, neck and neck with my bumper.

Across the lane I saw an angry face glaring at me. Even without formal training in lip reading, I recognized the words spewing from her mouth. (Certain phrases are universally understood.) She was even thoughtful enough to add a few hand signals so I wouldn't misunderstand her meaning.

Oh, come on, I thought. *Enough already.* When I looked over at her again, my disbelief turned to disgust. Sitting in the passenger seat was a young girl, no more than ten years old, staring out the window. Two rambunctious boys and another little girl, looking more humiliated than I felt, filled the backseat.

This wasn't a crazed teenager, but a mom, just like me, only she was having a temper tantrum.

Now *I* was angry. It's one thing to "act a fool" on your own time, but to "act a fool" in front of children? That's another thing. Chances were high that only two of the children belonged to this woman. The others were probably friends whose unsuspecting parents would be just as mortified as I was by this woman's irrational behavior.

Self-absorption in all its glory.

But that's not the end of our self-obsession. Not only do we want our own way, we want it ALL.

A restaurant once put out this sign:
THE BEST FOOD IN TOWN.
Indignant, the restaurant across the street posted another sign:
THE BEST FOOD IN THE STATE.

The first establishment responded with
THE BEST FOOD IN THE COUNTRY,
and the competitor came back with
THE BEST FOOD IN THE WORLD.
Finally, a small restaurant nearby brought
the contest to an end with its sign:
THE BEST FOOD ON THIS STREET.

BEN FRANKLIN[3]

WANTING EVERYTHING FOR OURSELVES (AND OUR CHILDREN)

The boom that followed World War II catapulted our economy into a buying frenzy. As we became more prosperous, we changed our definition of success. No longer was it defined by who you were, but by what you had.

In 1959, Victor Lebow, a retailing analyst, described the beginning of conspicuous consumption this way:

> Our enormously productive economy . . . demands that we make consumption our way of life, that we convert the buying and use of goods into rituals, that we seek our spiritual satisfaction, our ego satisfaction; in consumption. . . . We need things consumed, burned up, worn out, replaced, and discarded at an ever-increasing rate.[4]

The good you did for others in your community became secondary in importance to the good you did for yourself.

Luxuries became essentials.

Since 1950 the average new home has increased by 1,247 square feet while the average household has shrunk by one person.[5] In 2005 the National Association of Home Builders' average showcase home was 5,950 square feet, 15 percent bigger than the 2004 model.[6] The average new home requires 13,837 board feet of lumber and 19 tons of cement.[7] One in five new homes is larger than 3,000 square feet, the size at which it becomes unmanageable to clean without hired help.[8] One in four Americans wants at least a three-car garage.[9]

Today one in two homes have 2.5 baths or more compared to 1 in 100 in 1950.[10] Many of those bathrooms have multiple-head shower systems that can drain a forty-gallon tank in less than forty minutes.[11] One-third of a home's heating oil is used for hot water.[12]

Sales of "superpremium" refrigerators continue to rise by 15 percent yearly.[13] The average cost of a luxury kitchen remodel is $57,000. That's $10,000 more than it costs to build a typical Habitat for Humanity home.[14]

U.S. Consumer Spending in 2006 (Billions)[15]

- Clothing: $176
- Restaurants: $144
- Electronics/Appliances: $82
- Golf: $17
- Shoes: $22
- Florists: $6.6
- Casinos: $12
- Sporting Events: $22
- Furniture: $91
- Coffee shops: $4
- Doughnuts: $3
- Jewelry: $23

Fourteen million households own four or more televisions. Americans spend more to power home audio and video equipment that's turned "off" but still plugged in than they do to power such devices while actually in use.[16]

Since the coming of television, we no longer
have family circles—we have semicircles.
WISE OLD WILBUR

Imagine that we waste as much as we consume.

Sadly, our children learn that lesson from us early in life.

Last Christmas retailers offered our little ones some "essential" items for their choosing, including:

- A Luxury Coach for little girls priced at $47,000. This carriage promised to make every little princess's dreams come true. Handcrafted of wood and fiberglass, the oval-shaped interior measured just over six feet in diameter. Linens and interior options could be added upon request.[17]

- A Junior Off-Roader gasoline-powered vehicle for two, with a fully functional removable tape deck and speakers on both sides. For just $32,500 parents could get an early start teaching their seven- to twelve-year-old how to drive a car with this gas-guzzler. The car shifted into three different modes and had adjustable leather seats.[18]

- FAO Schwarz offered the world's largest piggybank, Wilbur the Pig. Parents could turn their child's room into a fiscal institution with this all-metal piggybank at the bargain price of $6,000. Wilbur was made from recycled aluminum and painted with nontoxic acrylic paint. Each came with a brass medallion and announced Wilbur's favorite phrase: "Some pig!" This extra-large pig was extremely heavy if filled with coins, weighing up to a thousand pounds.[19]

- The Tumble Outpost offered to turn backyards into Disneyland. This giant playset included a lookout tower with double rock-climbing walls, a fire pole, and a small play area. Kids could go on a great adventure over a swinging bridge on their way to the upper-level clubhouse or the jailhouse below. Other play features included a rope-net ladder, an earthquake landing platform, and a turbo-tube slide. The price tag? $97,510.[20]

No doubt someone will think of something "better" to offer our children next Christmas. No wonder kids have difficulty distinguishing the difference between a need and a want. We allow advertisers and marketers to tell them what they "need."

Expenditures for advertising and marketing aimed specifically at children have risen to over $15 billion a year. This amount is likely to grow with the increase in children's buying power, now estimated at more than $30 billion a year in direct purchases. It's estimated that the average child watches more than forty thousand television commercials per year.[21] We've put a new spin on the classic children's lullaby:

> Hush little baby, don't say a word,
>> Momma's gonna buy you a mockingbird.
> And if that mockingbird don't sing,
>> Papa's gonna buy you a diamond ring.
> But if that diamond ring turns brass,
>> Mamma's gonna buy you a looking glass.
> And if that looking glass looks odd,
>> Papa's gonna buy you a new iPod.
> And if that iPod's song gets stuck,
>> Mamma's gonna buy you a pickup truck.
> And if that pickup truck don't fly,
>> Papa's gonna buy and buy and buy.
> So, hush little baby, don't you cry.

While our children are shopping for the latest iPods, we're renting storage pods for our stuff and theirs. We used to outgrow our homes with the addition of more children; today we outgrow our homes with the addition of more things.

There was a time in our country when we yearned to have more time to read, do things with our friends, indulge in hobbies, spend more time with our children, go camping and travel. Instead, our work week hasn't shrunk, we are working longer hours than we did two decades ago. The tradeoff has been we are earning more money so we can buy more.[22]

How are we paying for our conspicuous consumption? The latest figures show American credit card debt in the $800 billion range. The average consumer has eleven credit cards carrying ten thousand dollars in charges.[23] A record 1.6 million Americans declared personal bankruptcy last year, while 60 million families shell out more than a thousand dollars a year just in interest and fees.[24]

We seem determined to teach our children the value of credit rather than the value of money. Companies are designing charge cards for kids, such as the recently announced "Hello Kitty" debit card with a target audience of ten- to fourteen-year-olds.[25]

Since 2001, the number of North Americans who have bought second homes has increased by 24 percent.[26] Not only do we need bigger homes for our stuff, but now we need second homes to escape from the stuff in our first homes. Could be it's not just our stuff we need to escape from; maybe we need to escape from ourselves.

After all, many of us can't seem to be content with simply being who we are. We want the world to know who we are.

WANTING TO APPEAR IMPORTANT

Imagine my reaction to the cover story of the January 1, 2007, issue of *Time* magazine: "Time Person of the Year—You. Yes, You. You Control the Information Age. Welcome to Your World." I couldn't have asked for a better introduction for this topic. The computer screen on the cover is a mirror so readers can see themselves when they pick up the magazine.

Why did the editors select "you" as the person of the year? Because "you" are the center of the universe. Users on YouTube upload sixty-five thousand new videos to the site every day. At the beginning of 2006 they watched ten million videos a day. By January 2007 the number soared to 100 million.[27] And that's just YouTube. I wouldn't even attempt a combined total for MySpace, Revver, Second Life, Bit-Torrent, LinkedIn, Flickr, and Blogger.

> The ideals which have lighted my way, and time after time have given me new courage to face life cheerfully, have been Kindness, Beauty, and Truth. The trite subjects of human efforts, possessions, outward success, and luxury have always seemed to me contemptible.
>
> ALBERT EINSTEIN

Daily writings once confined to locked diaries are now posted online for not only the nosy brother to read, but for the world to "enjoy." Private conversations kept secret from fear of embarrassment are open for input from strangers. Brian Williams, anchor and managing editor of *NBC Nightly News,* gave this explanation in an editorial found in the same issue of *Time:*

> We've raised a generation of Americans on a mantra of love and the importance of self as taught by brightly colored authority figures Barney and Elmo. On the theory that celebrating only the winners means excluding those who place, show, or simply show up, parents-turned-coaches started awarding trophies—entire bedrooms full—to all those who compete. Today everyone gets celebrated.[28]

With the rise of the techno age, we see folks desperately seeking to be special. Trouble is, such notoriety doesn't satisfy our need to be special. It only deepens it.

Dash, the indomitable superboy in the animated film *The Incredibles* pleads with his mom, Helen, to allow him to play sports at school. She tries to convince him that his superpowers combined with his superego make it impossible. In exasperation he says, "Dad said our powers were nothing to be ashamed of, our powers made us special."

"Everyone's special, Dash."

Grumbling under his breath, Dash sputters, "Which is just another way of saying no one is." [29]

But we want to be somebody special.

Paris Hilton, Nicole Richie, Britney Spears, and Lindsey Lohan spun out of control this year. Their quests to be someone important brought jail time, an out-of-wedlock pregnancy, divorce, and the revolving door of rehab. The more we want to be special in the eyes of society, the farther away we drift from a desire to please only God.

WHERE THIS HAS BROUGHT US

We are born with the desire to live according to our own rules, not God's rules. We long for recognition and awards, we long to be the center of our universe. We try to have it our way, but that only works with hamburgers. Living for ourselves just doesn't work.

A wise societal commentator once tried to warn us of the dangers of self-absorption. He wrote:

Don't love the world's ways. Don't love the world's goods . . . Practically everything that goes on in the world—wanting your own way, wanting everything for yourself, wanting to appear important—has nothing to do with the Father. It just isolates you from him. The world and all its wanting, wanting, wanting is on the way out. (I John 2:15–17, MSG)

These words were written centuries ago to folks just like us. They struggled with wanting the stuff the world offered them. They wanted multiple wives, jewels and bangles, and golden statues. Our stuff may look different (well, not all that different), but the temptations we face are the same: satisfying our sinful desires, acquiring all that we see, and "strutting our stuff," as my grandmother used to say. (She would literally squawk like a peacock if you bragged about yourself.)

The film *Wall Street* paints a sobering picture of where such desires lead us. Ruthless financial legend Gordon Gekko, portrayed by Michael Douglas, was attempting to persuade an unsuspecting boardroom full of Teldar Paper stockholders to vote in favor of his buyout offer. Little did they know, his aim was not to rescue the troubled company, but to destroy it and sell it off for a killer profit:

> The point is, ladies and gentleman, that greed, for lack of a better word, is good. Greed is right, greed works. Greed clarifies, cuts through and captures the essence of the evolutionary spirit. Greed, in all of its forms; greed for life, for money, for love, for knowledge, has marked the upward surge of mankind. And greed, you mark my words, will not only save Teldar Paper, but that other malfunctioning corporation called the U.S.A. Thank you very much.[30]

Gekko's words are chilling, aren't they? Yes, greed in all of its forms has not only "marked the upward surge of mankind" in this country, but the downward fall, too.

We would like to believe we're not greedy. We'd like to believe avarice doesn't control our lives. We'd like to believe we're above it, but we're not.

Never have been.

God gave the first couple all they would ever need to be "holy and happy" in the garden.[31] Holy, first. Happy, second. But they reversed the order, and that's what tripped them up. They wanted happiness before holiness. They missed God's truth that happiness comes from holiness, and so have we.

Look around. For the last forty years we have been doing all we can to put our own and our kid's happiness above all else. We've followed the advice of experts who told us that we need to help kids feel good about themselves. But look at where this has gotten us:

> Today's under-30s crowd has earned itself a nickname: Generation Me. Compared with older generations, young people today are increasingly displaying a lack of empathy, aggressive behavior and an inability to form relationships. At least that's the conclusion of a report from San Diego State University called "Egos Inflating Over Time." The study, conducted over a period of 25 years and based on interviews with more than 16,000 students, states that 30 percent more college students show "elevated narcissism" now than in 1982.[32]

But if this is true, and I believe it is, it's not our children's fault. It's ours. We've raised them to be self-focused rather then self-forgetful, self-serving rather than self-giving. We've taught them to esteem self rather than to esteem God. The fault is ours, but it's not too late to do something about it.

All that we seek and more can be found by accepting the gift of the Selfless Giver:

> And the Lord has declared this day that you are his people, his treasured possession as he promised, and that you are to keep all his commands. He has declared that he will set you in praise, fame and honor high above all the nations he has made

and that you will be a people holy to the Lord your God, as he promised. (Deuteronomy 26:18–19)

God can empty our self-centered hearts of self-destructive sinfulness and fill them with self-forgetful righteousness, and He can help us do the same for our children. Turn the page to find out how.

TWENTY YEARS OF WISDOM

1st year—I won't die from sleep deprivation.

2nd year—Tomorrow will be a better day.

3rd year—I *can* run faster than my child.

4th year—When I say no, only once with conviction, I win every time.

5th year—God gave children to parents, not parents to children.

6th year—Mom and Dad, not the children, set the rules.

7th year—If I listen with my eyes my children listen to me.

8th year—I really *do* need help in the kitchen with every meal.

9th year—I'm not perfect, so I cannot possibly raise perfect children.

10th year—My children will handle stress the same way I do.

11th year—My children mimic what I do, not what I say.

12th year—Boundaries keep pests out and my children in.

13th year—I encourage the best, praise the accomplishments, and forgive the mistakes.

14th year—My children will gain wisdom from their failures.

15th year—I am a capable, intelligent human being, no matter what my children think.

16th year—Maybe it *is* time for a cell phone.

17th year—I won't die from sleep deprivation during this stage either.

18th year—I cannot expect more of my almost adult than I do of myself.

19th year—I have to listen more, preach less.

20th year—It's time to let go with confident hope (and lots of prayer).

PART TWO

Bumping Your Child Off Self-Center

So here's what I want you to do, God helping you:
Take your everyday, ordinary life—
your sleeping, eating, going-to-work,
and walking-around life—and place it
before God as an offering.
Embracing what God does for you is the
best thing you can do for him.
Don't become so well-adjusted to your culture
that you fit into it without even thinking.
Instead, fix your attention on God.
You'll be changed from the inside out.
Readily recognize what he wants from you,
and quickly respond to it.
Unlike the culture around you, always dragging
you down to its level of immaturity,
God brings the best out of you, develops
well-formed maturity in you.

Romans 12:1 MSG

CHAPTER 3

Start Where You Are with a Parenting Plan

AFTER READING THE last chapter, you may be feeling a bit desperate—especially if your children are older, wondering if it's too late to turn the tide for your child. A woman called me just last week to say her eyes had been opened after reading the first few chapters of my book *Raising Respectful Children in a Disrespectful World*. She said her husband had been right all along. Her sixteen-year-old son, the apple of her eye, was stumbling. He was smoking, lazy, uninterested in life, and belligerent. She realized she had been parenting him out of fear—fear she would expect too much, so instead she had expected too little. She wanted to know if it was too late.

"No, it's never too late. Today is a new day," I told her. And I share the same message of hope with you. But you've got to take action now, and in this chapter we'll start at the beginning: (1) emptying your own heart of its self-centeredness, (2) accepting responsibility for your parenting so far, and (3) making a long-term parenting plan.

Do not conform any longer to the pattern of this world,
but be transformed by the renewing of your mind.
Then you will be able to test and approve
what God's will is—
his good, pleasing, and perfect will.
ROMANS 12:2

It's true that the older the child, the longer the recovery, but with God's help, parents *can* bump their child off self-center—no matter that child's age. A mother of a twelve-year-old confirmed this in a note to our office: "Since I've put into practice Ms. Rigby's suggestions, I have a happy and respectful child. It did not happen overnight; it takes work, love, and patience."

If you *think* you've blown it, or even if you *know* you've blown it, your spoiled ten-year-old son is more eager to forgive and forget than your ten-year-old Labrador. He wants you to train him using the same gusto with which you train your dog. (Not with the same treats, but with the same enthusiasm.) Your fifteen-year-old daughter wants you to help her avoid the pitfalls of living in a mirror. Underneath the clothes and makeup and the endless requests for more, she'd be happy to give it all up, in exchange for time with you. Not time spent in mindless busyness, but time spent learning together, growing together.

It doesn't matter if your children are tots, tykes, tweeners, or teens, you can begin emptying their hearts of selfishness, starting right now, with your own heart.

ASK GOD TO EMPTY YOUR OWN HEART OF SELF-CENTEREDNESS

If our own hearts are filled with selfishness, it's impossible to help our children cultivate unselfishness. Max Lucado's inspiring book, *Just Like*

Jesus,[1] reminds us that "God loves you just the way you are but he refuses to leave you there." God knows all too well the selfishness that lies deep within the human heart. He loves us so much that He can't wait for us to allow Him to empty our hearts of self-centeredness and to fill them with others-centeredness, like the heart of His Son.

How do you begin? By taking an honest assessment of your own self-centeredness.

Take the "Generosity Quotient Test"

Do you check the S&P 500 every day? Do you check the ups and downs of the NASDAQ? How about the NYSE US 100? Today I challenge you to check your GQ12 by taking the quiz below. Grab a pencil:

The Generosity Quotient Test

1. Do you tip the waitress or waiter with the same enthusiasm you order your food?

2. Do you complain when you have to fill in for your child's carpool due to another's schedule change?

3. If a friend needs you, do you willingly lay aside your plans to accomodate her/his needs?

4. Are you willing to give an egg, sugar, or other emergency ingredient to a neighbor in a cooking jam without expectation of return?

5. Are you willing to loan your tools to neighbors? And offer to help with their projects?

6. Will you watch your spouse/child's favorite television show at the expense of your favorite?

7. How do you treat solicitors at your door—with patience or curtness? (Girl Scout salesgirls, neighborhood children, window washers, lawn care, and so on.)

8. Do you make anonymous donations or do you give only when your name will be listed in print?

9. Are you willing to forgive your spouse when you've been inconvenienced? How many times did your fuss at your spouse this week over little nothings?

10. Are you willing to do undesirable tasks without complaining? (Pick up dry cleaning, stop on the way home for a gallon of milk, and so on.)

11. Do you go the extra mile for the adults in your children's lives? (Coaches, teachers, school bus driver, etc.)

12. Are you willing to work in the concession stand at your child's game, even though you despise it and would rather be in the stands?

How'd you do? Did you discover you're more invested in yourself than others?

If so, let me encourage you to do "the 139." Several years ago God showed me the power of praying Psalm 139 as a way of inviting Him to remove the selfishness from my heart.

Do the "139"

I was part of a women's Bible study that met once a week for more than twelve years. We cried together, laughed together, and prayed together. We walked through untimely deaths of spouses, unwanted divorces, and wayward children. We studied individual books of the Bible, in-depth studies, and classical Christian writings. We assessed each other's strengths and weaknesses. We encouraged and exhorted each other. Together we worked hard at letting go of our self-centeredness and need to control our spouses and children. Our desire was to deepen our relationships with God and to mature in our relationships with our spouses and children.

The most effective prayer we found for emptying our hearts of selfish desires came from the closing verses of Psalm 139: "Search me, O God, and know my heart; test me and know my anxious thoughts. See if there is any offensive way in me, and lead me in the way everlasting" (verses 23–24). If a prayer request for a spouse turned into a complaint fest, one of us would remind the complainer to do "the 139." If a woman requested prayer for the resolution of a conflict with a child, we reminded Mom to start with "the 139." As we prayed this prayer, God began to transform our selfish hearts into selfless hearts, and we were able to turn conflict into conversation.

So, if you are worried about your shortcomings and inadequacies or that you're not "good" enough to bump your children off self-center because of your own selfishness, do "the 139"! When you pray these verses, you are telling God you trust Him to help you. What a joy and a relief for Him.

He knows your heart better than you do. He knows who you are and who you are meant to become. He looks at you with eyes of love and mercy, not condemnation. He wants to free you from the bondage of self-centeredness. But the process does not always feel good. You will become aware of the little things you do that are selfish—the ill-spoken word, wrong attitude, critical tone of voice. God delights in showing us where we're missing the mark, because He longs to set us in the right direction. His searchlight penetrates the deepest crevices of our hearts to reveal those "little things" we rationalize or excuse in ourselves. While this can be painful, it's necessary if we want to raise selfless children. Even more, it's necessary if we want to become the people God wants us to be. I've seen husbands and wives use these powerful verses as their daily prayer. Homes filled with individuals wanting their own way have been transformed into homes

PART TWO: BUMPING YOUR CHILD OFF SELF-CENTER

filled with family members wanting to serve each other. Your home can be this way too! Start where you are by doing "the 139."

Once you've asked God to empty your heart of self-centeredness, you must be willing to accept responsibility for your duties as a parent.

ACCEPT RESPONSIBILITY

There comes a time when parents can no longer blame society, the media, the next-door neighbor, their children's friends, or the school-teacher if their children aren't fitting in. Just ask Tom.

He didn't just love his son, he worshiped him. In Tom's eyes, Will could do no wrong, and so Tom stood up to teachers, friends, and neighbors who dared to criticize his son. Will's first-grade teacher tried to tell his father there would be trouble ahead, but he didn't listen. (Or perhaps, he didn't want to hear her "been there, done that" advice.) By the time Will finished elementary school, he had earned a reputation as a competitive kid who refused to settle for being number two at anything.

Middle school became a testing ground for Will's competitive spirit. As he moved into a feeder school with new and older kids, Will's drive to be on top went into hyper mode on the soccer field. Tom enjoyed his son's aggressiveness and continued to encourage him to be number one. When other players complained about Will's attitude on the field, Tom brushed it off as jealousy.

Will had become all that Tom programmed him to be. But this father recognized he'd made a mess of things the day the soccer coach called him and his son in for a conference in order to tell them that Will would be kicked off the team if he continued to resist being a team player.

Tom realized that he was responsible for Will's inability to get along with other kids and even adults. As they left the coach's office, Tom put his arm around his son's shoulders and asked his forgiveness.

He took responsibility for his son's arrogance and promised from that day forward he would change his perspective and help his son change his point of view, no matter how difficult.

But if Tom (or any parent) is going to fulfill this promise, he has to have a plan.

DEVELOP A PARENTING PLAN

Parents without a long-term plan for their children are a little like Alice in *Alice in Wonderland*:

> In a conversation with the Cheshire Cat, Alice asked, "Would you tell me please, which way I ought to go from here?"
>
> "That depends a good deal on where you want to get to," said the cat.
>
> "I don't much care where," said Alice.
>
> "Then it doesn't matter which way you go," said the cat.[2]

We can desire to raise unselfish children, but if we don't have a plan for how we're going to do it, we'll have a hard time reaching our destination. Along the way, Mom will go crazy, Dad will be crabby, and the kids will be cranky.

We wouldn't launch into a new business venture without a well-written business plan. We wouldn't think of building a new home without blueprints, nor would we travel from Portland, Maine, to Portland, Oregon, without a road map. In the same way, we must intentionally, rationally, emotionally, and wholeheartedly seek to raise unselfish children, or it won't happen.

That's why Brian and Jerrie LeDoux made a decision before their children were born that they were going to be parents first, friends second. Jerrie and Brian lead a focused life with their three children: Sarah, Carlin, and Morgan. Their parenting plan is simple: to raise godly children who know who they are and Whom they serve. Selfishness doesn't fit into the plan, but integrity does.

When I asked Jerrie to tell me about their parenting plan, she said:

I taught my children the meaning of *integrity* when they were very young. To me, integrity means to do the right thing simply because it is right. So when my kids were young I found ways of catching them doing "right" and then I made mention of it. (I don't believe in rewarding kids with things for a job well done, but I do congratulate them.)

Part of our plan was to build a strong sense of family identity. We are the LeDoux family. We have taught our children the way *we* expect them to behave. We never foster self-indulgence. We don't allow others to define what that looks like or how we should be as a family. We feel it's okay to say to our children, "Our family doesn't do that because . . ."

We've also made it clear to our children that we don't have to give them a reason for our decisions beyond the fact that we make decisions in their best interest. When our children could understand the concept of God (around the age of five), I explained that if they didn't learn to obey me, they wouldn't learn to obey God. I wanted them to grow up with the conviction that even though God doesn't give us a reason for His decisions, we can trust Him because He always has our best interest at heart.

> Any child can be taught to be beautifully
> behaved with no effort greater than quiet
> patience and perseverance, whereas to break bad
> habits once they are acquired is a Herculean task.
> EMILY POST

A unique aspect of the LeDoux, parenting plan is their take on the teen years:

> We have taught our children that the Jewish system of adult-hood at thirteen is more correct than our society's notion of delayed maturation. Our children have responded well to our expectation that when they reach thirteen, they behave as an adult, and they appreciate the benefits that come with mature behavior.

The word *teenager* didn't appear in the dictionary until 1938.[3] Up until then, children were expected to go directly from childhood into adult-hood. There wasn't a stage called *adolescence*. There wasn't a period of exploration between childhood and adulthood. At thirteen children took on adult responsibilities. I recently met a couple who married when she was fourteen. They had just celebrated their seventy-sixth anniversary. (You'll meet them later in the book.) Today, we're telling twenty-five-year-olds they're too young to marry and sustain a lifelong commitment. Now, I'm not suggesting that you allow your children to get married at fourteen, but we've got to admit that as parents, we generally promote self-indulgence in the teen years.

But if your goal is to start a revolution in your home, if you want to raise children who become responsible adults who give to others, let me suggest that you make the following commitments:

1. *Make a commitment to God to raise your children to be others-centered rather than self-centered,* which means throwing away the mirror and living at the window. (See chapter 6 for ways to develop God-confidence in your children.)

2. *Make a commitment to your spouse to live with less in order to enjoy more.* Rid yourself of self-indulgent habits. Find joy in

simple pleasures. Think of the example you can set before your children if you skip the four-dollar cup of coffee or the weekly manicure and instead give the money to a worthwhile cause that benefits those who can't afford a four-dollar pack of hamburger meat.

3. *Make a commitment to faithfully and joyfully tithe.*

4. *Make a commitment that enough will be enough.* Don't buy the latest gadgets for yourself or your children. Prove to the rest of the world that there's much more to life than things. Make a home that appreciates the little things and doesn't need the big things.

5. *Make a commitment to family togetherness.* Replace the emptiness of going, going, going with playing, playing, playing. Children don't need activities six days a week if they find fulfillment within the family. They don't have to find ways to satisfy themselves when they find satisfaction in the relationships within their family. (We'll talk more about how to ensure this in chapter 8.)

Home—
A place where the little things are so precious,
the big things aren't noticed.
WISE OLD WILBUR

If you are feeling a bit overwhelmed right now, let me assure you that you don't have to figure this out on your own. God is right beside you to teach you, set you straight, help you set personal and family limits, and train you for the task He has given you as a parent.

REMEMBER WHERE TO GO FOR HELP

God will never turn His back on you or your children. Remember, you're on the top of His priority list. Even if you are parenting in less-than-perfect conditions, even if you didn't have a good role model in your own parents, God can help you overcome those limitations.

God's Instruction Manual

In fact, He's even given you an instruction manual: the Bible. If you'll read it and study it, you'll find that parenting to raise self-forgetful children is easier than you might think. Remember, "All Scripture is God-breathed and is useful for teaching, rebuking, correcting and training in righteousness, so that the man of God may be thoroughly equipped for every good work" (2 Timothy 3:16–17).

Following are a few key passages to get you started in your study and application of God's Word. Here you'll find help in how to *teach, rebuke, correct,* and *train* your children in righteousness so that He can accomplish His purpose in their lives.

1. *To be able to teach your children God's ways, you must study His Word. Proverbs says:* "If you accept my words and store up my commands within you, turning your ear to wisdom and applying your heart to understanding, and if you call out for insight and cry aloud for understanding, and if you look for it as for silver and search for it as for hidden treasure, then you will understand the fear of the Lord and find the knowledge of God." (2:1–5)

2. *To be able to* rebuke *(reprimand) your children, you must live with integrity.* Integrity and respect go hand in hand. If you want your children to respect you, you must be respectable. Paul admonishes: "Get rid of all bitterness, rage and anger, brawling and slander, along with every form of malice:

Be kind and compassionate to one another, forgiving each other, just as in Christ God forgave you." (Ephesians 4:31–32)

3. *To be able to* correct *(discipline) your children, you must be filled with humility, not pride.* Your children need to know that you are their authority only because God is your authority. It's not because "I said so," but because "God said so": "All of you clothe yourselves with humility toward one another, because God opposes the proud, and gives grace to the humble. Humble yourselves, therefore, under God's mighty hand, that he may lift you up in due time." (1 Peter 5:5–6)

4. *To be able to* train *(guide), you must walk your talk.* If you're selfish rather than generous, or tightfisted rather than openhanded, your children will be too: "Don't be misled: No one makes a fool of God. What a person plants, he will harvest. The person who plants selfishness, ignoring the needs of others—ignoring God!—harvests a crop of weeds. All he'll have to show for his life is weeds! But the one who plants in response to God, letting God's Spirit do the growth work in him, harvests a crop of real life, eternal life." (Galatians 6:7 MSG)

Let me also recommend that you study Proverbs and Ecclesiastes. The first nine chapters of Proverbs address tots to twenty-somethings. Chapters 10 through 24 offer timeless wisdom for all of us. The final seven chapters, 25 to 31, present important principles for leaders, whether in the home, the workplace, or community. In addition, Ecclesiastes can help you see God's truth when it comes to the long-lasting value of earthly possessions.

Not only does Scripture give us insight for how we can bump ourselves and our children off self-center, it also contains stories of powerful role models for how moms and dads can model selflessness to their children.

Motherhood According to Hannah

Hannah's husband, Elkanah, loved her dearly, but, as polygamy was customary in biblical times, he had a second wife, Peninnah.[4] Peninnah may not have had Elkanah's love, but she had his children. Hannah desperately wanted children but remained childless. She suffered in silence while she watched Peninnah give birth numerous times.

For one week each year, the "family"—Elkanah, Hannah, Peninnah and all her children—made a pilgrimage to Shiloh for a time of worship and sacrifice. Not a cozy family vacation for Hannah, was it? I can't imagine a more difficult week for Hannah, yet she selflessly honored her husband and went along without complaint.

Peninnah used this holiday celebration to ridicule and laugh at Hannah. Elkanah showed great tenderness toward Hannah, offering his undivided attention during the feast to soothe her misery. But the pain of her barrenness and Peninnah's relentless mouth overwhelmed Hannah to the point of tears. At the conclusion of the feast, Hannah fled to the tabernacle to find solace with God.

She knew that God had "closed her womb" and that He alone could give her a child. She prayed, "O, Lord Almighty, if you will only look upon your servant's misery and remember me, and not forget your servant but give her a son, then I will give him to the Lord for all the days of his life, and no razor will ever be used on his head." In contemporary terms, she was saying, "Give me your gift, Lord, and I will return the gift to you." She was willing to give her child back to God, if He would only allow her the pleasure of bearing a child.

Eli, the priest, witnessed Hannah's desperate plea and assured her, "Go in peace, and may the God of Israel grant you what you have asked of Him." Having poured out her heart before God, Hannah returned home in peace.

God heard Hannah's cries. Within the year, she gave birth to a son, naming him Samuel, which means "heard from God."

Hannah devoted herself to Samuel. She kept him close, protecting and preparing him for his time of dedication to the Lord. When he was between the ages of three and five, Hannah and Elkanah returned to Shiloh. Hannah approached Eli, saying, "As surely as you live, my lord, I am the woman who stood here beside you praying to the Lord. I prayed for this child, and the Lord has granted me what I asked of him. So now I give him to the Lord. For his whole life he will be given over to the Lord."

Hannah fulfilled her promise to God and left Samuel under the tutelage of Eli, but her obedience, daily prayers, and years of devotion helped him grow up to become Israel's greatest judge, bringing order out of chaos to Israel.

What can we learn from Hannah about being unselfish mothers who raise unselfish children?

1. *Model selflessness by not allowing difficult circumstances to make you bitter.* Hannah was miserable at times, but she never allowed her sadness to turn to bitterness. Hannah remained devoted to her husband in spite of difficult circumstances.

    We're so spoiled in today's culture that many wives consider a difficult circumstance having to turn their husband's socks inside out before they do the wash. Instead, allow your husband's annoying habits to become the little quirks that make him unique. Hannah chose not to complain and we can, too, especially in front of our children. Have you ever noticed that moms who complain usually have children who complain? Whiners beget whiners.

2. *Model selflessness by trusting God with your children.* Hannah ran to God, not in anger, but in angst. He was the only one

who could bring her peace. She knew He could make the impossible possible. Knowing she would have to love Samuel from afar, she willingly gave her son back to God out of gratitude.

Hannah's example encourages us to raise our children to serve God, which brings glory to God and honor to our children. Helping our children find God's purpose for their lives is more important than what we think. We need to stay in prayer for God's wisdom as we seek to guide our kids.

3. *Model selflessness by giving without the expectation of return.* Hannah gave to her family without thought of herself. She didn't look to others to fill her soul, but instead allowed God to do His miracle work in her. Even though her time with Samuel came to an abrupt halt, her heart stayed with her son and she continued to give to him, even though there was no immediate "payoff" for her efforts. She even tailored a new robe for Samuel as a symbol of her love. We, too, can cover our children with our love.

Mom, let Hannah be your inspiration for giving unselfishly to your family. Allow God's love to pour through you to your spouse and children. Dedicate your children to the Lord's service, whatever His plan might be for their lives.

> Raising children God's way brings glory to
> God and honor to your children.
> WISE OLD WILBUR

Fatherhood According to Joseph

When Joseph learned that his fiancée was pregnant, he had the legal right to divorce her or even have her stoned to death for her "indiscretion." Yet he refused to publicly embarrass her. The tenderness Joseph

Dad, give your son a special gift
on his wedding day . . .
God's definition of success tucked
inside a family Bible.

Dear [*your son's name*].
Be strong and courageous, because you will lead
your family to inherit the land
God promises to give them.
Be strong and very courageous.
Be careful to obey all the law God has given you;
do not turn from it to the right or to the left,
that you may be successful wherever you go.
Do not let this Book of the Law
depart from your mouth;
meditate on it day and night, so that you may be
careful to do everything written in it.
Then you will be prosperous and successful.
Has God not commanded you?
Be strong and courageous. Do not be terrified;
do not be discouraged,
for the Lord your God will be with you wherever
you go (adapted from 1 Chronicles 28:20).
Given with much love from your earthly father,
on behalf of your Heavenly Father,
Dad

gave Mary in the midst of his great disappointment showed his deep love for her.[5]

An angel appeared to Joseph in a dream and said, "Joseph son of

David, do not be afraid to take Mary home as your wife, because what is conceived in her is from the Holy Spirit. She will give birth to a son, and you are to give him the name Jesus, because he will save his people from their sins." Without hesitation, Joseph put fear and anger and disappointment aside and took Mary as his bride. He accepted without question the role he was to play in God's plan.

Joseph had a deep, abiding faith that didn't question God. He was more concerned about protecting his wife and son than he was about what others would think of his decisions.

Under his watchful eye, Jesus matured into a strong and wise young man. Can't you imagine Jesus at the workbench learning from his father, a master carpenter? Jesus learned to build furniture and repair broken oxcart wheels long before he learned to repair broken hearts. We're told that "Jesus grew in wisdom and stature and in favor with God and men" (Luke 2:52).

What can we learn from Joseph about being unselfish fathers who raise unselfish children?

1. *Model selflessness through self-sacrifice.* Joseph was willing to be criticized and hassled by others in order to obey God. In today's self-absorbed society, it's all too easy to listen to other people's definition of success. Don't listen to those voices. Listen to God's voice. Be a caring husband, a patient father, a man who gives your best at home, not just at work. Be a man who plays as hard with his family as he does with his buddies and a man who loves God more than he loves himself.

2. *Model selflessness by displaying courage.* Merriam-Webster's defines courage as "mental or moral strength to venture, persevere, and withstand danger, fear, or difficulty." Courage is also bravery, valor, conviction, and tenacity. Joseph showed tremendous courage by following God's com-

mands. He was unwilling to allow Mary to be disgraced. He stood by her in the face of his own humiliation. (Read the book of Hosea for another look at a man called by God to a hard place.) Just as Joseph was the protector of his family, be a humble warrior for your wife and children. They need your gentle touch at home while you fight for them outside the home.

3. *Model selflessness by loving your wife.* The greatest act of self-lessness you can show your children is to love their mother "just as Christ loved the church" (Ephesians 5:25). Allow your children to see your affection for each other and to see you putting her needs before your own. Don't let anything come between the two of you.

Parents, if you want to give your sons and daughters the best of everything, start with the best of yourself. Parents who give a lot can expect a lot. Parents who are unselfish in their relationships and transactions with others, who give generously to others, and who show great mercy when wronged will raise giving children. When parents get it right, their kids are more likely to get it right.

With God's help, you can raise unselfish children. It's never too late to do the right thing, even when it comes to being a parent. So, ask God daily to empty your heart of selfishness, accept responsibility for your parenting mistakes, and help you make a parenting plan, that starts today, to raise unselfish children. Most important, always remember to rely on God for help.

CHAPTER 4

Take Charge of Your Child

Aᴍᴀssᴀᴄʜᴜsᴇᴛᴛs ᴄᴏᴜᴘʟᴇ ᴀɴᴅ their three-year-old daughter were returning from a Florida vacation on an Air Tran flight when their daughter refused to take her seat for takeoff. When the flight attendants insisted the girl had to be buckled up, she had a "you're not the boss of me" tantrum. The parents asked for more time to talk with their daughter. (Remember, she was three!) The kicking and screaming continued. Fifteen minutes later the attendants asked the family to leave the plane because the child refused to be buckled up.

I absolutely agreed with this decision. Why? Because these parents did not take charge in this situation by placing their obstinate three-year-old in her seat and buckling her up, no matter how loudly she howled or how wildly she kicked.

In the aftermath the major networks covered the story. Talk radio had a field day, along with late-night comedians. The media criticized the airline, but many of us saw it differently. Air Tran released a statement three weeks following the event, stating that 92 percent of the e-mails and phone calls they had received supported their decision.[1] However, while most parents can see that what these parents were doing was wrong, they overlook similar errors in their own parenting choices.

In one way or another, many parents are not taking charge in their role as the parent. *SuperNanny*, a popular television show featuring Jo Frost as nanny to the rescue, features families that are out of control because parents are not in control. The few episodes I've watched depicted parents who were too preoccupied with their own "stuff" to discipline their children, or who bought every new toy on the market in hopes that it would make up for their lack of time with their children, or who did everything for their kids from tying their shoes to doing their homework, thus keeping them from learning necessary life skills. In every case the parents were sabotaging their children by not giving them what they really needed.

THREE TYPES OF PARENTS

My work with families and children has led me to conclude there are at least three types of parents. Only one of these types takes charge of their parenting role, which in turn helps to bump their children off self-center.

Deflector

Deflector Parents "deflect" their role as parents onto their children by asking their kids to make decisions they are not yet capable of making. This sends children the harmful message that they are the boss and prevents them from learning to accept authority.

Depriver

Depriver Parents "deprive" their children of what they need either by:

1. *Doing too little.* These self-absorbed parents make little or no time for their children, depriving them of the love and

attention they need from their parents. These parents often use "things" as a substitute for relationship. As a result, their children grow up to be self-absorbed adults who constantly try to feel better about themselves and are incapable of forming authentic relationships.

2. *Doing too much.* These self-deceived parents do everything for their children, sometimes out of a desire to make their children happy, other times because it is easier for the parents to do it themselves. They deprive their children of opportunities to learn necessary life skills, making it difficult for them to mature into capable adults. Instead they grow up to be self-absorbed adults who think others are there to serve them.

Developer

Developer Parents "develop" children by giving them what they need when they need it. As a result, these children grow up to be the capable and responsible adults God created them to be.

———

Deflectors and Deprivers are not doing what they can to help their children become balanced, mature young adults. They're more concerned with their own happiness, or with keeping peace, or with their children's happiness. In contrast, Developers zero in on the needs of their children. Their goal is to help their child make a difference in the world by finding his or her place beyond the window.

In order to help you determine your own parenting type and what you might need to change in order to take charge of your role as a parent, let's take a closer look at each of these, beginning with Deflector Parents.

DEFLECTOR PARENTS
DON'T TAKE CHARGE AS NEEDED

Madeleine's mom is a Deflector. The following scene depicts a typical morning in their household.

———————

"Good morning, honey," Mom says to three-year-old Madeleine as she waddles to the breakfast table, half awake, half asleep. "What kind of cereal would you like? We have Cocoa Puffs, Cheerios, Rice Krispies, Froot Loops, Frosted Flakes, or Cinnamon Toast Crunch."

"I want Lucky Charms," mumbles Madeleine.

"Sweetie, we don't have Lucky Charms."

"I don't want cereal."

"Okay. How about toast and eggs?"

"Okay."

"Do you want wheat bread, white bread, or raisin bread?"

"I want plain bread."

"You want your eggs scrambled or fried?"

"Cooked good."

"Cooked good toast and eggs, coming right up! What flavor milk this morning . . . plain, strawberry, or chocolate?"

"I want orange juice."

"Okay, orange juice it is. Your eggs are almost ready," Mom says in a cheerful voice.

"I'm not hungry," wails Madeleine as she leaves the table and curls up on the sofa.

"Get over here right this minute and eat your breakfast! I don't stand here and cook because it's fun, you know!"

"I don't want to!"

"Madeleine Marie, get over here right this minute!"

"You're not the boss of me!"

Exasperated, Mom moves on to Madeleine's older brother: "Andrew, what would you like for breakfast?"

———

Madeleine was telling it like she saw it and experienced it. Mom was *not* the boss of her. *Madeleine* was the boss. Truth is, when children say "you're not the boss of me," they're right to one degree or another. Not because the child has taken control, but because the parent has deflected his or her parental role onto the child.

Madeleine's mom believed she was helping her daughter, but she wasn't. Madeleine didn't want to be the boss. Madeleine just wanted some "cooked good" food—it really didn't matter what, but if Mom was going to force her to make decision after decision, Madeleine was going to be difficult.

Children aren't capable of making decisions, even simple decisions about what to eat or what to wear, until they are at least four years old. At three years old, Madeleine *needs* Mom to be in charge. Underneath, she *wants* Mom to be in charge. Children look to their parents for answers. Yet Deflector Parents, instead of giving children answers, *ask* them questions, and then wonder why their children question everything they say.

> Today's children are out of control,
> because parents are not taking control.
> WISE OLD WILBUR

Two things can happen to children who are being pressured to make decisions they are incapable of making:

1. They feel overwhelmed and shut down, as Madeleine did, or

2. They feel frustrated and have a full-blown temper tantrum.

It also feeds the child's innate selfishness by sending a message to the child that says his or her opinion is the only one that matters. Remember, your goal is to bump your children off self-center, not keep them in the center of their universe.

DEPRIVER PARENTS DO EITHER TOO LITTLE OR TOO MUCH

Substituting "Things" for Love

Julie, now in her mid-twenties, grew up with a father who spent long hours at the office or traveling for business and a mother who was very involved in community work, often leaving her young daughter with a caretaker. In order to make themselves feel better, both parents constantly lavished their daughter with gifts.

When Julie turned twelve, her parents gave her a credit card, and were always telling her, "Go buy yourself something pretty." It wasn't that her parents didn't love her; they did. But they didn't want to interrupt their own lives for their daughter's sake.

When Julie entered high school, she realized her parents were giving her "pretty things" as a substitute for their time and attention, and resentment toward her parents began to fester in her soul. To mask her resentment, the by-product of neediness and insecurity, Julie developed an air of arrogant confidence. As her resentment grew, her self-absorption grew. The parents she so dearly loved refused to focus on her, so she focused on herself.

Because her parents were depriving her of a nurturing relationship with them, Julie sought to nurture herself in other ways. In order to lessen the pain of her parent's lack of interest in her life, she participated in extracurricular activities that didn't require her parents presence—studying, sex, and shopping. In order to feel special, Julie pushed herself to achieve. She tried to earn her parents' affection by getting good grades and excelling in whatever she did. She didn't just want to be perfect, she *needed* to be perfect in hopes that her parents would be so impressed that they couldn't help but notice her. In order to feel close to someone, Julie had fleeting sexual encounters, but these only left her feeling emptier. She tried to fill the gaping hole in her heart with lots of pretty things. In just one shopping trip she used her parents' credit card to buy three pairs of shoes, two dresses, makeup, five pairs of earrings, and a new cell phone. By her senior year, her shopping wasn't limited to the weekends; she shopped on weekdays, too.

Julie's now working on an advanced degree. Because Julie's an overachiever who appears to function well, outward appearances seem to say that her parents did a pretty good job of raising their daughter. From the inside looking out, however, things don't look so good. Emotionally, Julie has the maturity of a fifteen-year-old. She's volatile, hard to please, and self-absorbed. Her insecurity causes her to attempt to buy her way into friendships by pulling out the "plastic" to pick up the tab. She doesn't have real friends, because underneath the façade, she doesn't know how to cultivate a genuine relationship with anyone. Deep down, she's very lonely.

Julie's parents deprived her of what she needed most—a loving relationship with them. As a result she wasn't able to mature emotionally. She didn't learn how to argue constructively or how to give and take in relationships. She was never able to express her emotions in healthy ways.

Depriver Parents who use things as a substitute for a relationship with their children, raise kids who look in the wrong places to fill the emptiness.

Confusing Overinvolvement with Genuine Love

John grew up with a mom who suffered from the "perfect mom" syndrome. She waited on her children twenty-four hours a day. I was astonished when eleven-year-old John asked his mom for a snack while she and I were visiting one afternoon. She jumped up to accommodate his request. Five minutes later, he called out, "Mom, I need a drink." She again jumped up to accommodate her son's request. Not once in the three hours I was there did John lift a finger to take care of himself. When suppertime rolled around, Mom prepared the meal without asking for her son's assistance. I asked my friend why, and she said it was her job to take care of her kids and their job to be a kid.

While my friend may sound like she is modeling selflessness by doing so much for her son, who was capable of getting himself a snack and doing regular chores around the house, in actuality she was telling him that others are there to serve him.

Can you imagine the teenager he will become? I expect he'll be much like the lazy teen I saw in the Denver airport.

The luggage carousel started spinning in the terminal, dropping bags from our flight. Travelers huddled around to grab their bags. I noticed a woman and her teenage son waiting with the rest of us. The young man stood back a bit, plugged into an iPod, while his mom watched for their luggage.

Mom reached for a large black duffle bag and then strained to pick it up, but the son didn't flinch. The same thing happened when another of their bags came around, and again the teenager didn't move. When Mom reached for the third bag, a gentleman standing nearby pushed past the young man to assist his mother, giving the boy a look that said it all. The teenager glared back with a look that offered *his* opinion of the stranger's opinion. The gentleman turned to the mom and said, "Ma'am, you better do something about your boy or one day somebody else will."

A HOME MAY BE EITHER—

An inspiration or an agitation.
A dream or a nightmare when memory writes
its records on the tablets of the heart.
A place where children may
Do or where they must DON'T.
A haven of rest or a whirlpool of dissatisfaction.
A center of cheer or a dumping
ground for grouches.
A sunbeam in a sorry world or a
thundercloud in a summer sky.
A place of greatest use or the
poorest excuse of a place.
A fertile field of growth or a desert of stagnation.
A harbinger of hope or a hangman of despair.
A place to flee to or a place to flee from.
But any home, be it high or humble,
is exactly what you make it.
AUTHOR UNKNOWN[2]

What does John's mom and this mom have in common? They may love their children, but in doing everything for them, these moms are crippling their children. Their children are consumed in their own little worlds, because they don't have to participate in their parents' world.

Depriver Parents who do too much for their kids not only teach them to focus on themselves, they also fail to help their children learn necessary life skills, such as cooking, cleaning, and money management.

DEVELOPER PARENTS TAKE CHARGE

Remember Madeleine and her mom? What might that scenario have looked like if Mom had been the boss when it came to what Madeleine ate for breakfast? Take a look:

———————

"Good Morning, honey," Mom said to three-year-old Madeleine as she waddled to the breakfast table, half awake, half asleep. "Having trouble waking up this morning? I bet a bowl of Froot Loops and toast with your favorite strawberry jam will wake you up."

"Can I have Lucky Charms?" asked Madeleine.

"It'll have to be Froot Loops this morning, your bowl is ready."

"Okay."

"Here you go, honey," Mom said, as she put Madeleine's breakfast in front of her. Five-year-old Andrew, already dressed for preschool, sat down next to his sister.

"Good morning, Andrew. Would you pour the juice, please?" asked Mom.

"God is good. God is great. Thank you for the plate," prayed Madeleine.

Mom and Andrew giggled at her error, but they didn't say a word.

"Andrew, here's your favorite grape jam for your toast," Mom said.

Madeleine looked over at Andrew and made a profound observation, "I like strawberry and you like grape. You're a boy and I'm a girl!"

———————

In the above scenario, Mom is in charge. She makes the decisions for her family from a heart that cares. Even though Madeleine asks for

Lucky Charms, Mom serves her Froot Loops. She's not heartless, though, she offered both children their favorite jam selections. When Andrew came to the table, she asked him to serve the juice, a responsibility that a young child can manage.

Your children learn how to make decisions by watching your decision-making process. Parents ask too much of children when they expect a three-year-old to decide what she will eat for breakfast, which outfit she would like to wear, or if she would like to invite a friend over. *Children need parents who make decisions for them until they're mature enough to make decisions for themselves.*

The following chart can serve as a general guideline for how many decisions parents should be allowing their children to make themselves.

Percentage of the Decisions Made by the Child

Age	Birth to 4	5 to 8	9 to 11	12 to 15	16 to 19
Percentage	0%	20%	40%	50%	80%

The ability to make decisions happens in incremental steps, based on a child's age and maturity. Children mature at different rates, according to their innate abilities and personalities, but here is an overview of what kinds of decisions you should allow your children to make at each stage of their development.

1. Birth to Age Four

Until your children are five years old, you should make 100 percent of the decisions regarding:

Clothes. You should select their clothes, without soliciting their input.

Food. You plan the menus, taking into consideration your children's favorite foods, but also introducing them to new foods. If they don't want to eat the supper you have prepared, don't give them something else to eat instead. Your kids won't starve before the next morning, and after they leave a meal hungry a few times, they will soon to learn to eat whatever you serve them.

Television/movies. Take charge of what programs your kids view and for how long. I recommend limiting television viewing to no more than thirty minutes a day at this age.

Bedtime/nap time. Be in control of the bedtime/nap time schedule. I'm a proponent of schedules because a schedule makes the household run smoothly and predictably, which allows children to feel secure.

Toys. Take control over the toys that your children play with. Make sure they are age appropriate. For example, a four-year-old girl shouldn't have a Bratz doll (in my opinion, no little girl should have one), and a three-year-old boy isn't ready for a science kit.

Young children can learn decision-making skills by watching your choices. You can also begin to teach them good decision-making by reading and talking with them about the decisions characters make in classics such as *Pinocchio, The Ant and the Grasshopper, The Little Red Hen, The Three Little Kittens, The Princess and the Pea, The Emperor's New Clothes, The Three Little Pigs, Chicken Little, William Tell,* or *The Little Engine That Could.* These stories are as engaging to young children today as they were when I was a child. They maintain their power to convey truths to your children that will be remembered.

2. Ages Five to Eight

Allow five-, six-, seven-, and eight-year-olds to make about 20 percent of the decisions regarding:

Clothes. Give children a choice between two outfits.

Food. Plan the menu for meals, keeping your kids in mind, but allow your children to choose what they will eat for a snack from your selection of choices.

Television/movies. Let your children choose which shows to watch within your selection of age-appropriate choices. Take control of the amount of time allowed for viewing. I recommend thirty minutes up to an hour for five- to six-year-olds. No longer than an hour for seven- to eight-year-olds.

Bedtime/nap time. Bedtime is still your domain. You decide what time kids this age go to bed. At this age they need a few minutes of down time after they've had their nighttime ritual with you. Most children don't need to nap at this stage, but I recommend that parents require children this age to rest quietly in the afternoon for an hour. Your children can decide whether they will sleep, read, or rest during this time. No playing allowed.

Chores. Give children this age some assigned duties (see pages 81–89 for more about this).

Toys. Let your children choose between your choices of age-appropriate toys.

3. Ages Nine to Twelve

Allow nine-, ten-, eleven-, and twelve-year-olds to make 40 percent of the decisions regarding:

Television/movies/Internet. Your children can choose what movies or television shows they watch. However, don't allow them to view PG-13 movies, and reserve the right to say no to any movie or show that doesn't meet with your approval. You still control the time allowed. I recommend one hour a day for this age group.

Mealtime/menus. This is the time to begin to teach your children cooking skills. Allow them to choose the menus, per your approval, and to help you with the meal preparation.

Bedtime. While you should still determine the time, your kids can choose the order of things. Some children prefer a bath right after supper. Others enjoy downtime before bathing. It's most helpful for all if a routine is established and followed during school nights.

Clothing. Allow children this age to choose what they wear when, as long as you have approved of the clothes at the point of purchase.

Homework. Let your children decide when they'll do their homework. For instance, whether it will be before or after dinner. Some children come in from school ready to get homework out of the way. Others need downtime and become more productive after supper. Either way, homework must be completed by bedtime.

Duties. Children this age can choose when to complete their duties, but you should still assign the duties and enforce consequences if the duties aren't carried out within the established time frame.

Church. Don't allow your children to decide whether they will attend church. This is nonnegotiable. Keep in mind that much of their attitude about church at this age is dependent upon yours. If Sunday morning is pleasant and you're not complaining or arguing, your children won't either.

4. Ages Thirteen to Fifteen

Allow thirteen-, fourteen-, and fifteen-year-olds to make 50 percent of the decisions regarding:

Television/movies/Internet. Teens will insist on making their own choices, but R-rated movies are nonnegotiable. Same is true with the Internet. It's your choice which sites are appropriate. You can prohibit your teen from viewing television, movies, or the Internet if he or she has homework or a poor attitude.

Mealtime/menus. Ask your children to choose the menus for mealtimes, to grocery shop, and to prepare one meal a week—or more, if they enjoy cooking.

Clothing/makeup. This is the time for parents to instill in their children the understanding that clothes tell who you are; they can invite trouble or help you avoid trouble. Clothes tell the world how much or how little you think of yourself. The same is true for makeup. Your teen can choose his or her clothing with the understanding that your veto is just as powerful as the president's.

Duties. Expect teens to maintain their assigned responsibilities within the family. Don't back off on consequences if they fail to fulfill their duties.

Church. I know opinions vary greatly on this issue, but I believe that as long as your children live under your roof, the rule should be: "As for me and my house, we will serve the Lord."

5. Ages Sixteen to Nineteen

Allow sixteen-, seventeen-, eighteen-, and nineteen-year-olds who are still living at home to make 80 percent of the decisions regarding:

Television/movies/Internet. Your seventeen-year-old has the "right" to walk into an R-rated film at a movie theater, but you are still in charge of what goes on in your home. You can limit your teen from viewing television, video, or the Internet if he or she has homework to do or a poor attitude.

Clothing/makeup. Allow teens this age to decide how they will portray themselves to the world. Their choices in this area will reflect how they view themselves. Pay attention . . . don't argue, but guide with grace and empathy.

Duties. Expect teens to maintain responsibilities within the family, but allow them to negotiate with you concerning the "what and when."

Curfew. At the onset of this stage, curfew is your call, but with each year, allow your teen to negotiate the terms. By the senior year in high school, your teen should be responsible for setting his or her own curfew, as long as you know where your teen is going and what time he or she will be home. If your teen sets an unreasonable curfew, you have the right to refuse it. You still have to give final approval while your teen is living under your roof. If your teen comes in at 3:00 in the morning on Sunday, he or she still has to roll out of bed for church. Your teen will quickly learn how to set a reasonable curfew.

Church. If your teen has started college but is still living at home, expect your child to attend church with the family. Kids who are enjoying the benefits of being at home should participate in the family's worship.

Keep in mind this important principle: If you're modeling good decision-making by your choices, your children will be more likely to learn to do the same. If you are not, keep reading. You'll need to stop your destructive choices for the sake of your children.

I began this chapter with a story about a couple who didn't understand their role as parents. I want to end with the story of a dad in a similar situation who understood his role as parent and took charge of his child and the situation.

A DAD WHO UNDERSTOOD HIS ROLE AS PARENT

A few weeks after the story of the Massachusetts couple and their daughter appeared in the news, I was flying home from Colorado and noticed a young couple and two small children. The little boy, probably five years old, became increasingly antsy and irritated as he sat next to his mom. He wanted to sit with his dad, who was seated in the row behind the boy with his older sister. (The truth of the matter was that the little boy was tired of sitting.) After a few minutes of negotiation, Mom and Dad agreed to the child swap.

The little boy was ecstatic. His sister didn't seem to mind; she was immersed in a book she was reading. The switch was made, all was well—until the little boy decided he didn't want to sit down. He wanted to stand on the seat and jump up and down and entertain the rest of us.

My first thought, *Not again. I can't believe I'm seeing this firsthand.* But what followed was a shining moment of parenthood. Dad reached up for his son, who energetically protested, but Dad sat him down in his seat anyway, and said, "Son, I'm just as tired of sitting as you are. Everybody on this plane is tired of sitting, but until this plane lands on the ground, we all have to sit, and that includes you. Now, let's find something we can do while you sit here with the rest of us."

Outstanding! I looked at the woman sitting next to me, who was taking it all in, too. We nodded in approval at each other.

Dad knew who was in charge, and his son knew it, too. The rest of the flight was without incident. Upon departure, I stopped the couple to compliment their great parenting. Dad responded, "If there's one thing I can't tolerate, it's parents who let their kids run the show. It makes everybody around them miserable, including the kid."

Dad was right.

WHAT KIND OF PARENT WILL YOU BE?

Now that you've read this chapter, you have a decision to make. What kind of parent will you be? A Deflector Parent, who refuses to take charge of your duties, deflecting your responsibility and forcing your children to be in charge before they're ready? A Depriver Parent, who gives too much or too little, without regard for your children's needs, while depriving them of the ability to mature and take charge of their own lives one day? Or will you be a Developer Parent, who takes charge of his or her role as parent?

I'm hoping that if you're not doing so already, you'll begin the process of developing your children, helping them grow into the selfless young men and women God intends them to be. We'll spend the rest of this book exploring how you can do just that.

CHAPTER 5

Meet All Their Needs, But Not All Their Wants

H AVE YOU EVER met anyone who doesn't have a soft spot for Opie Taylor, Sheriff Andy's adorable son on *The Andy Griffith Show?* He was a fine young man with a father who really did know best. Go back with me to a 1963 episode titled, "Opie and the Spoiled Kid,"[1] to learn a lesson or two from a father who had no problem bumping his son off self-center.

Arnold Windler, a kid much too big for his britches, and his family are new residents of Mayberry. Arnold and Opie have an interesting exchange about Arnold's new bike, the latest model Intercontinental Flyer . . .

Opie to Arnold: "Boy, it's a beauty. How much did it cost?"

Arnold: "Seventy dollars."

Opie: "Gosh, you must have been saving up for it since you was a kid."

Arnold: "My dad bought it for me."

Opie: "For your birthday or something?"

Arnold: "Oh, no, I save my birthday for something big."

Opie: "What's bigger than an Intercontinental Flyer?"

Arnold: "Gillions of stuff . . . a pony, a boat, all kinds of stuff . . . what ya' doing?"

Opie: "I didn't get my twenty-five cents this week yet. I'm cleaning out the garage."

Arnold: "You get twenty-five cents for this big job?"

Opie: "Oh, no. I take out the ashes, keep the woodbox filled, and set the table every night."

Arnold: "Oh, boy, did your old man see you coming."

Opie: "What do you mean?"

Arnold: "He's taking advantage of you."

Opie: "I don't know what you're talking about."

Arnold: "You're not *supposed* to *work* for your allowance. What do you think allowance means? It means money the kid is allowed to have. And without working for it. It's for being a kid."

Opie: "Are you sure? Seems to me like Pa would have told me if that's so."

Let's pick up with Opie as he confronts Andy with this new information . . .

Opie: "Are there rules for how a Pa should treat his son if he's a kid?"

Andy: "Rules, what rules?"

Opie: "The rule that kids get paid seventy-five cents a week allowance without working for it."

Andy: "The seventy-five-cent rule? I haven't heard of that one. Seventy-five cents and no work, huh? You want it straight, don't you? There are no rules for Pas and sons. It's as simple as this . . . each mother or father raises his boy or girl, as the case may be, the way he thinks is best. And I think it's best for you to get a quarter and work for it. You see, when you give something, in this instance, cleaning the garage, and you get something in return, like a quarter, that's the greatest feeling in the world. You do feel good after working, don't you?"

Later in the episode, Barney and Andy catch up to Opie's new friend, Arnold Windler, running over folks on the sidewalk with his fancy new Intercontinental Flyer. After giving Arnold a fair warning, which he ignored, they impound his prized possession. You can imagine his reaction. "I'm going to tell my father about this. He'll get my bike back."

Arnold and his father stormed into the sheriff's office, demanding the return of the bicycle. When Andy refused, Arnold went on a rampage. Opie stood by in stunned silence as Andy gave Mr. Windler a fatherhood lesson . . .

Arnold's father: "He's a good boy . . . really . . . a little high-spirited perhaps. But weren't we all at his age?"

Andy: "If we don't teach children to live in society today, what's going to happen when they grow up?"

Arnold's father: "For heaven's sake. The boy's not a criminal."

Andy: "I didn't say he was. What he does at home is none of
our business. But when he gets out on the street, he is
going to have to answer to us."

Mr. Windler had fallen into the trap of giving his son the things he
wanted rather than teaching him the lessons he needed.

What do your children really *need* from you? Love, guidance, shelter, food, clothing, medical care, and an education. That's it. Everything else is a *want*, a luxury: video games, iPods, cell phones, the latest
fashion—whatever new item their friends have.

Today, far too many parents fall for the "nag factor." They know
their kids are bombarded by ads telling them to buy certain products
and that many parents are buying those products for their children. They know the pressure that comes from their children's peers,
and so they buy their kids far more "stuff" than they can even use, all
in the hope that their children will fit in and be accepted by their
peers.

According to a recent survey of youth commissioned by the Center
for a New American Dream, the average twelve- to seventeen-year-
old who asks a parent for products will ask nine times until the parents finally give in. For parents of tweens, the problem is particularly
severe—more than 10 percent of twelve- to thirteen-year-olds admit to
asking their parents more than fifty times for products they've seen ad-
vertised.[2] Kids have learned if they nag enough for long enough, parents will give in.

Parents, stop falling for the nag factor.

In early childhood you may lay the
foundation of poverty or riches,
industry or idleness, good or evil,
by the habits to which you train your children.
Teach them right habits then, and their future life is safe.
LYDIA SIGOURNEY (1791–1865)

REFUSE TO OVERINDULGE YOUR KIDS

Sadly, our self-absorbed society has told parents to help their kids feel good about themselves, that it's the parents' duty to make their children happy. But underneath it all, kids don't need parents who make them happy. They need parents who will make them capable.

Dr. Connie Dawson, co-author of *How Much is Enough,* writes: "When parents give children too much stuff that costs money, do things for children that they can do for themselves, do not expect children to do chores, do not have good rules and let children run the family, parents are overindulging."[3]

Here are some other signs of overindulgence. As you read them, watch for your weak spot:

1. Overindulging children is giving them things or experiences that are not appropriate for their age or their interests. For example:

   • Allowing a five-year-old to dress like a pop star

   • Allowing a twelve-year-old to watch an R-rated movie

   • Removing curfew from a sixteen-year-old with a new driver's license

2. Overindulgence is giving things to meet the adult's needs, not the child's. For example:

   • A mom buying her daughter the trendiest clothes, because Mom believes it's a reflection on her own style

   • A dad giving his son the "stand out" wheels at sixteen, so Dad's friends—as well as his son's friends—will think he's "the man"

- A parent giving his or her children the best of the best in order to make the parent look successful

3. Overindulgence is giving too much and expecting too little. As pointed out earlier, doing and having too much too soon prevents children from maturing and reaching their full potential. For example:

  - Not requiring your four-year-old to make requests using "please," or not requiring "thank you" from your five-year-old for simple kidnesses

  - Giving unlimited computer time to your tween without requiring duties to be performed first

  - Funding your teenager's weekends—giving him or her money for gas, movies, or other entertainment—instead of expecting the teen to earn his or her own spending money

4. Overindulgence is neglecting to teach your children the life skills they need to survive in the "real" world beyond your home. For example:

  - Tying the shoes and dressing four-year-olds who are perfectly capable of dressing themselves

  - Not expecting tweens to prepare their own lunch during the summer months

  - Doing the laundry for teenagers who are more than capable and need to learn to do it for themselves

Did you find your weak spot? I admit that I slipped into overindulgence in raising my sons in more than one area. It's important to realize the harm this can do to our children. According to one study conducted in 2001, children who are overindulged are more likely to grow up to believe the following:

1. It is difficult to be happy unless one looks good, is intelligent, rich, and creative.

2. My happiness depends on most people I know liking me.

3. If I fail partly, it is as bad as being a total failure.

4. I can't be happy if I miss out on many of the good things in life.

5. Being alone leads to unhappiness.

6. If someone disagrees with me, it probably indicates that the person doesn't like me.

7. My happiness depends more on other people than it depends on me.

8. If I fail at my work, I consider myself a failure as a person.[4]

So, for the sake of your children, stop overindulging them.

Instead, teach them the difference between a need and a want, and then make them work for their wants. For instance, rather than buying that new video game for your children, give them two options: Tell them they can place it on a wish list for a birthday or Christmas present, or they can do extra duties to earn the money to buy it themselves. If your children are willing to work for their "heart's desire," they'll take better care of it, be more grateful for it, and think long and hard before turning a "want" into a "need" in the future.

Parents can begin to remedy the damage done by overindulgence by doing two things:

1. Helping their kids cultivate patience.

2. Giving children opportunities to develop responsibility and to feel valuable.

Let's take a look at each of these.

HELP THEM DEVELOP PATIENCE

The truth is parents often *prevent* their children from learning patience. We've gotten just as caught up in our fast-food society as anyone else. We've forgotten that real life problems aren't solved in fifteen minutes, that it takes time to find solutions to everyday struggles. We're the ones who try to speed things up for our kids.

So don't be so quick to solve your children's problems for them. A bit of a struggle is good for them. Just ask Reverend Harold Wilke, a minister who was born without arms and is an advocate for the disabled. He tells the following story about how his mother refused to solve all his problems, because she knew that her son needed to learn to solve them on his own.

I was two or three years old, sitting on the floor of my bedroom trying to get a shirt over my head and around my shoulders, and having an extraordinarily difficult time. I was grunting and sweating, and my mother just stood there and watched. Obviously, I now realize that her arms must have been rigidly at her side; every instinct in her had wanted to reach out and do it for me.

Finally, a friend turned to her and said in exasperation, "Ida, why don't you help that child?" My mother responded through gritted teeth, "I *am* helping him." [5]

This wise mom knew that her son needed to know what he was capable of doing himself, and that he wouldn't ever learn that unless she refused to rescue him.

No matter the age of your child, you can create opportunities for him or her to learn patience. Here are some age-appropriate ideas to get you started:

Tots (from birth to three years old)

- Offer compliments when he or she demonstrates patience. This will motivate your child to develop more patience.

Tykes (from three years old to six years old)

- If your tyke gets into a quarrel with a friend, don't intervene too quickly and send the other child home. Wait. Give the children time to resolve it themselves, unless they begin hitting. If that happens, step in and separate them until they can come together without conflict.

- Teach them to count to ten while thinking through their actions before they act. Explain the consequences of impatience. For example: teach them that doing something in anger can damage a friendship.

- On Christmas morning, insist that everyone is up and around the tree before any presents are opened.

Tweens (from six years old to twelve years old)

- If your six-year-old struggles to read a big word, rather than tell him or her the word, which would be quick and easy, help your child sound it out s-l-o-w-l-y.

- Read a chapter a night with your children from a classic, like the Narnia series. This enables kids to learn the thrill of anticipation, looking forward to the unfolding of the next piece of the story. They learn to wait and use their imaginations in the waiting!

- Have your children start a long-term project that will take weeks to complete. For example, put together a 1,000-piece jigsaw puzzle, build a rocket, plant a garden, or build a treehouse.

- Keep books with you at all times. Pull them out when the line becomes too long and give them to your kids to read.

- Teach your children that different situations call for different behavior. For example, tell them that it's okay to run to the fridge at your house, but not at a friend's house. Train them to wait patiently to be offered food or drink in someone else's home.

Teens (from thirteen years old to nineteen years old)

- Encourage your teen to work hard to excel at something. Becoming proficient at a sport or a musical instrument or hobby takes a lot of time and patience, but the rewards will be great for your teenager.

- Put teens in charge of planning the next family vacation or large purchase. Let them take charge of the details—gathering the information, comparing prices, and determining the best value for the dollar.

- Your teen can cultivate patience by saving money for a special purchase. Watching a nest egg grow is patience in action.

One more thing: always remember the value of modeling patience. Don't only use your words to teach your children patience. Show them patience by being patient with yourself and others.

Now let's see how you can cultivate responsibility and a sense of value in your kids.

GIVE THEM OPPORTUNITIES TO LEARN RESPONSIBILITY

Your children need your help if they are going to learn necessary life skills. They need you to give them regular chores or duties and to hold them accountable for taking care of those duties. In so doing, you will help your children become adults, not just grown-ups.

All children will at times engage in a power struggle when it comes to carrying out chores or duties. But if parents give in and don't assign age-appropriate duties for their children, their kids will grow up to be irresponsible, which is heartbreaking for the parent and tragic for the children. No matter the age of the child, any duties you assign them should encompass these purposes:

- Helping your child learn life skills.

- Helping your child become a valuable member of the family.

- Helping your child become a valuable member of society.

By giving your children opportunities to help and serve each other within the family, you're preparing them to take care of themselves and go out and serve society.

Parents with lots of kids must learn to do this out of necessity. To help you learn how to delegate duties to children at all age levels, I've gleaned some suggestions from several families with at least six children. All of them stressed two things:

1. The importance of "show and tell" when it comes to assigning duties. It's not enough to tell children to carry out a

task; *parents must take the time to show them how to do it.* (This is why some parents indulge their kids—it is easier for the parents to do something themselves than to take the time to teach their children how to do it.) If you don't teach your kids how to execute the task, it's your fault if they aren't successful at carrying out the task. Lack of successful completion creates frustration in children because they want to perform their tasks well.

2. The need to hold children accountable for accomplishing the task.

Let's get started by getting our children started.

Tots (From Two to Three Years Old)

Are you wondering what duties you could possibly expect of a two-year old? The goal is to introduce the concept of duty by helping tots find satisfaction in accomplishing simple tasks. Young children have a strong desire to please. You can build on that desire by allowing them to help you.

Two-year-olds are capable of organizing their room or "space" to accommodate their belongings. "Tell" your children what you they are supposed to do while you "show" them how to do it. Walk your children through how to pick up their toys and place them in the proper place.

Additional duties for tots include:

- Putting away their shoes

- Putting dirty clothes in the laundry hamper

- Throwing away their own diapers

- Sharing their toys with siblings and friends

82

Tykes (From Three Years Old to Six Years Old)

As children grow, their duties grow with them. Children need to experience being a part of something greater than themselves. When parents give children duties that only they perform, those children experience the satisfaction of having something of value to contribute to the family.

If you have shown your child how to fulfill a duty, accept your child's best effort without redoing his or her work. You can't expect a four-year-old to make a bed as well as you do.

Personal duties for tykes include:

- Dressing themselves

- Brushing their teeth

- Brushing their hair

- Making their own bed when they get up

- Tying their shoes

Family duties for tykes:

- Placing their cups/plates/bowls at the sink

- Washing fruits/vegetables

- Exercising good manners

- Helping to fold the laundry and take it to their room

- Picking up sticks in the yard

Tweens (From Six Years Old to Twelve Years Old)

If you're still doing tasks for your children that they are capable of doing, STOP. Not only do you need to let them carry out these tasks, at times you also need to allow them to fail at fulfilling their duty,

TIPS FOR SUCCESSFUL DUTY TRAINING

- Model responsible behavior when it comes to your own responsibility.

- Give encouragement, not criticism.

- Accept your children's best effort.

- Remember to "show and tell."

- Decide ahead of time the consequence for not fulfilling a duty, and communicate that consequence to the child.

- Remind only once, then follow through with the consequence.

- Don't offer tangible rewards; allow intrinsic rewards.

- Maintain your patience.

- Tell your children no when no is the best answer.

even if this causes problems for them. If children don't ever experience the natural consequences of their failure to carry out their duties, then they won't learn the valuable lesson of not being defeated by failure.

My son Chad was a forgetful third-grader until the day he found out he would have to rely on himself, not his mom's willingness to rescue him, to remember his schoolwork. One Monday morning, he again forgot to take his schoolwork to school, even though I'd reminded him and his brother to check their backpacks for all needed schoolwork.

Just as Chad jumped out of the car, he remembered the papers he had left on his desk at home. "Mom, will you pleeeeeeeeeeeeeease go get my math sheet? I don't have class until ten this morning. Thank you, Mom," he said, walking away from the car with all the confidence in the world that it would be taken care of. But this time I responded with a statement he had not heard before, "No, Chad, I won't do that today."

Chad had not learned his lesson, but I had learned mine. It was time for him to suffer the consequences of his forgetfulness and to learn that it was *his* responsibility, not mine, to pack his backpack and remember his homework.

You would have thought by his reaction that I had told him to kiss his brother! His tantrum rivaled the most horrific tantrums I've seen from two-year-olds. Of course, it took place in the carpool line in front of other moms dropping off their angels. I drove away with tears puddling in my lap, watching my son being pulled back on the sidewalk by a teacher. I circled the block, wanting to return to ask him to forgive me, but I knew in my heart this was best for Chad, even though he would receive a zero on his homework assignment.

When I returned to pick him up that afternoon, Chad had obviously surmised that his best course of action was silence. We "kissed and made up" at supper. I didn't apologize, but I did give Chad a big hug and told him, "I love you."

"Yeah, I know, Mom. I love you, too."

You already know without me saying it—Chad wasn't forgetful again. And he learned an important secondary lesson: he found out Mom wasn't meant to be his servant but his helper.

Our children can't learn responsibility if we're serving them rather than helping them.

Personal duties for tweens include:

- Making their own school lunches

- Cleaning their rooms

- Managing their time wisely

- Engaging in some extracurricular activity, such as music lessons or being involved in a sport

- Managing the money they receive as an allowance. (It's common for parents to connect their children's allowance with the fulfillment of their duties. I don't recommend this, because duties should be performed by members of the family. However, you can encourage your kids to earn extra money by doing extra jobs. Be sure to tell your children you are giving them an allowance so they can learn the necessary life skill of money management.)

- Completing their homework on time

- Showering/personal hygiene

Family duties for tweens:

- Washing the dishes

- Putting away the groceries

- Setting the table for meals

- Watering the indoor plants

- Taking out the garbage

- Sweeping the porch/deck

- Raking leaves

- Making their own lunches

- Gathering schoolwork/packing backpack

- Feeding the family pet

- Dusting the furniture

Teens (From Thirteen Years Old to Nineteen Years Old)

The transition from home to the world begins in this stage of development. This is the time to assign duties equal to the privileges your teen requests. For instance, if your seventeen-year-old son wants to use the car, he should be responsible for cleaning it, inside and out. If your thirteen-year-old wants to spend the night at a friend's on Friday night and come home late Saturday afternoon, she'll have to find a way to complete homework and duties. (Teens may dislike your requirement of fulfilling duties, but they'll thank you for it later.)

By the time your children graduate from high school, they must be prepared to take care of themselves apart from your help and without your supervision.

Personal duties for teens include:

- Paying part of their own car insurance

- Paying for the gasoline they use

- Participating in an extracurricular activity

- Working in a part-time job

- Doing their own laundry

- Maintaining the car they drive, whether the family car or their own

  - Refilling oil

  - Checking air in tires

- Washing the exterior

- Cleaning the interior

Family duties for your teens:

- Mowing the lawn

- Babysitting younger siblings

- Planning/preparing meals

- Grocery shopping

- Household jobs, such as:

  - Vacuuming

  - Cleaning bathrooms

  - Changing light bulbs

  - Changing sheets

  - Taking out the trash

  - Washing and ironing their clothes

  - Clearing the table and washing the dishes

  - Cooking a meal once a week for the family

I'll never lie to you . . . I'll always tell you the truth.
I'll encourage you when you *want* it,
but I'll push you when I know you *need* it.
Onnie Jordan

Now that I've asked you not to overindulge your kids with their wants, I want to encourage you to overindulge them with love, real love. Love that molds and shapes them into the young men and women they are meant to become. Patiently help them develop patience, and with persistence and persuasion give them age-appropriate responsibilities. As you do these things, you'll be preparing their hearts and minds to accept the responsibilities God has planned for them.

CHAPTER 6

Nurture God-Confidence

LYDIA PLAYFOOT, A sixteen-year-old student in London, lost her battle to wear her purity ring at school. The British High Court ruled that wearing the ring violated a school policy banning jewelry. Allowances were in place for students of other religions to wear items integral to their faith, but the court argued that the purity ring was not part of the expression of Christianity.

In response to the ruling, Lydia said: "I am very disappointed by the decision this morning by the High Court not to allow me to wear my purity ring to school as an expression of my Christian faith not to have sex outside marriage. I believe that the judge's decision will mean that slowly, over time, people such as school governors, employers, political organizations and others will be allowed to stop Christians from publicly expressing and practicing their faith." [1]

Lydia has plenty of God-confidence. She knows who she belongs to and Who she's fighting for. She knows what she believes, and she is willing to take a stand for her beliefs. The battle she waged was not for herself, but for God. Her confidence in Him gave her the courage to fight for the rights of Christians to freely express their faith.

Fourteen-year-old Carlin is another young person who grew up with parents who nurtured God-confidence in him. They taught him that all of his gifts had come from God and to use his gifts to serve God and others.

Carlin has played Dixie Youth baseball since he was old enough to swing a bat. He's a talented player who has been an asset to his teams over the years, but his humility makes him a delight to be around. His parents earn a comfortable living, but they don't have money for extras, like buying their son several custom bats or expensive cleats. Carlin doesn't mind, and up until a year ago, it wasn't a problem for anyone else on his team.

A year ago Carlin moved into a new league with boys who have a different outlook on life. One day after a successful game in which Carlin had made a difference in the outcome, he slipped off his cleats and put on his tennis shoes. His teammates noticed his cheap, "no brand" tennis shoes and started ragging him about them. Carlin stood up, turned to the guys on the bench, and quietly yet firmly said, "Hey, it's not where you get your shoes that matter, it's where your shoes take you that counts."

Carlin knows who he is and where he is headed, and because of this he was able to kindly put his peers in their place. He wasn't arrogant about it, but he wasn't timid either. Carlin doesn't need to fit in. He knows what is really important in life, and it's certainly not the approval of others. I'm willing to bet that many of his teammates will remember his words when they move into adulthood not knowing where they're going.

God-confidence is:

- Knowing who you are and Whose you are

- Not thinking more highly of yourself than you should

- Choosing to be obedient to God, regardless of what it costs

- Accepting your call from God

Our self-absorbed society tells young people, "Do something and be somebody!" God says, "You *are* somebody; now do *your* something."

Our self-absorbed society says, "Take all you can get, and you will get more!" God says, "Give all you have, and you will receive."

Our self-absorbed society says, "Hate your enemies, run over people, climb to the top!" God says, "Love your enemies, help people, be a servant leader."[2]

If we want our children to grow up to be humble adults who place their confidence in God rather than in themselves, we must:

- Teach them to listen to God's voice.

- Help them see His hand in their lives.

- Give them opportunities to serve God by serving others.

- Teach them that their gifts come from God.

> Humility before God gives confidence before men.
> WISE OLD WILBUR

HELP THEM LEARN TO LISTEN FOR GOD'S VOICE

What are your children listening for? The phone to ring? The release of the next CD by their favorite group? The announcement of the new techno gadget? The voice of God? The first three "calls" are hard for them to miss, just by virtue of their volume. That last call comes just as often, but God doesn't yell to get our attention. He whispers.

That's likely why Samuel had a hard time recognizing God's voice and why he needed help to know it was God calling his name (see 1 Samuel 3).

During the years Samuel lived in the temple under Eli's training, God rarely spoke directly to His people. It was a time in Israel's history that the people were led by judges, without a king. One night

Samuel was sleeping when he heard his name called. Thinking the call came from Eli, he answered and went immediately to Eli. But Eli said, "I did not call; go back and lie down." So Samuel returned to his rest.

Again, Samuel heard his name called and went to Eli. Again Eli said, "My son, I did not call; go back and lie down." A third time Samuel heard his name and returned to Eli's side.

Eli realized it was the Lord calling Samuel and said, "Go and lie down, and if he calls you, say, 'Speak, Lord, for your servant is listening' " (3:9).

Samuel did as Eli had instructed and God told Samuel of impending disaster coming to Eli and his sons. This was the beginning of Samuel's lifelong practice of listening for God's voice and answering His call. Samuel grew up to become Israel's last and greatest judge.

How can you help your children listen for God's voice, so they don't miss it?

1. *Teach them that God speaks to us, and that we need to listen to what He says.* Read the story of how God spoke to Samuel with your children. Point out that Eli helped Samuel discern God's voice, just as you're helping them learn to do. Help them memorize Samuel's response to God's call, "Speak, Lord, for your servant is listening" (1 Samuel 3:9). With older kids, you can talk with them about times when you have heard God's voice, and why you believe the voice was God's and not from your own mind.

2. *Help them see how God speaks to us in His Word.* Since we know that God has spoken to us in His Word, this is the most obvious place to start listening to what He has to tell us. As a family, read and memorize Scripture together, so that your children begin to recognize God's voice. (Third-graders are old enough to memorize the books of the

Bible.) One of the first Scriptures I taught my sons was 2 Timothy 3:16–17: "All Scripture is God-breathed and is useful for teaching, rebuking, correcting and training in righteousness, so that the man of God may be thoroughly equipped for every good work."

I wanted my boys to know that God has already told us many things about who and Whose we are, as well as how we are to live in this world.

For example:

- "You are a chosen people, a royal priesthood, a holy nation, a people belonging to God, that you may declare the praises of him who called you out of darkness into his wonderful light." (1 Peter 2:9)

- "God created man in his own image, in the image of God he created him; male and female he created them." (Genesis 1:27)

- "O Lord you are our Father. We are the clay, you are the potter; we are all the work of your hand." (Isaiah 64:8)

- "We are God's workmanship, created in Christ Jesus to do good works, which God prepared in advance for us to do." (Ephesians 2:10)

- "It is God who works in you to will and to act according to his good purpose." (Philippians 2:13)

Children who memorize Scripture will be better prepared to discern God's voice when they're torn between God's voice and the voice of others. Kids who know God's Word and how to navigate it are more likely to check what others are saying against the truth in Scripture.

3. *Teach your children that God is the only One we kneel before.*
Every night during prayer time, kneel with your children in
prayer. When your children are young, be sure to explain to
them why you are kneeling, and why we only kneel before
God. Read together the story of Shadrach, Meshach, and
Abednego in Daniel 3, as well as other stories of people
who refused to bow before anyone other than God. Two of
my favorites include:

- Daniel, who refused to pray to anyone but God and
found himself in a den of lions. (Daniel 6)

- Mordecai and Esther, who saved the Jewish people from
extinction, ignored the protocol of the King's court,
risking Esther's life. (Book of Esther)

4. *Teach your children both sides of prayer, talking and listening.*
One of the ways I've done this over the years is to tell children the following true story of a man who understood the
importance of listening for God's voice in prayer.

Jim's Prayer

"It's Jim," the man prayed aloud as he knelt before the altar.
Early morning sun poured through the windows in the beautiful old chapel to welcome the guest.

Jim came by the church every day. Every day he walked
past the receptionist at the entrance door, kindly nodded to
her, and then slipped into the chapel. Some days he only stayed
a few short minutes. Other days he stayed as long as an hour.

One day the pastor approached Jim as he was leaving the
chapel. The pastor wanted to invite Jim to become a part of
their congregation, but the only thing he knew about this man
was his name, so he said, "Jim, we're honored that you come

by so often. We'd love to have you become a part of our church family."

Jim replied, "Thank you, Pastor, but I'm a member of a congregation at a church across town. I'm working a half-night shift on a construction job down the street from here, so I come in during my breakfast hour to check in."

"Check in?" inquired the pastor.

"Yes, Sir. I can't hear God out there, and I need to know what He needs me to do, so I come in here to check in with Him."

Jim understood the importance of listening for God's voice in prayer. Children who grow up with parents who teach them to listen for God's voice will, too.

When my sons were little, one of the ways I did this was to encourage them to listen to God in prayer during our nightly prayer time. After we finished the "bless everybody and everything" part of our prayers, we then asked God questions, such as, "Would you show me someone to help at school tomorrow?" or "I don't know how to stop the kids from bullying me, would you give me your answer?" I would encourage the boys to listen for an answer as they were going to sleep and when they woke up. The next morning I would remind them to watch and listen. I was amazed and amused at how often they came in from school with a "Mom, Mom, you won't believe this" story of God's faithfulness.

In middle school and high school, I asked them, "What did God say?" if they announced they had made a decision about an issue they were grappling with. Or I would ask, "Did you ask God about it before you made a decision? He might have a different opinion than you do." We also checked decisions against God's Word. If the decision didn't square with God's Word, I encouraged them to allow God's Word to be the final word!

The voices of the world only get stronger as our children grow older, pulling them into pursuits that feed their self-centeredness, telling them "it's all about you." The greatest protection we can give them is the ability to hear God's voice and the desire to obey Him, which begins as soon as they're old enough to say, "God."

Dr. Albert Schweitzer's theology was a bit controversial in his day, but when he was asked to write a message to children in a book about heroes, he rightly emphasized the importance of listening for God's voice:

> Tell the boys and girls that the truths they feel deep down in their hearts are the real truths. God's love speaks to us in our hearts and tries to work through us in the world. We must listen to this voice. We must listen to it as to a pure and distant melody that comes across the noise of the world's doing. Some say, "When we are grown up, we will listen. Now while we are young, we would rather think of other things." But with the voice of Love, with which God speaks to us in the secret places of the heart, God speaks to us when we are young so that our youth may be really youth, and that we may become the children of God. Happy are those who listen.[3]

Yes, happy are those who listen.

Life is not what the world says, but what God says.
It's not about self-discovery, but God-discovery.
It's not finding the answers,
but knowing the One who has the answers.
It's not making ourselves important,
but making God important.
It's not how good we are, but how good God is.
It's not feeling good about ourselves,
but knowing God feels good about us.

It's not about self-fulfillment, but self-denial.

It's not having self-esteem, but Christ-esteem.

It's not loving ourselves, but loving God.

It's not loving ourselves, but loving others.

It's not receiving awards on earth, but rewards in heaven.

WISE OLD WILBUR

God-confidence comes not only from listening to God's voice, but also from seeing His involvement in our lives. How, then, can you help your kids see God's hand in their lives?

SHOW THEM GOD'S HAND IN EVERYDAY CIRCUMSTANCES

Several years ago my Sunday school students were coming into class with stories of "coincidences" from their week. I wanted to help these sixth-graders recognize God's hand in their lives. I wanted them to be able to see Him in the details of their lives and see that He works around us to create circumstances to bless and enable us to bless others, so I prayed for an abundance of God-incidences I could share with the kids.

The following Sunday I told them about two incidents where I had seen God at work during the week. The first time was when I'd written someone's name on my "To call" list, only to have that person walk in and sit next to me in a meeting later that same day. The second time was when I forgot one item at the grocery store, went back in, and "bumped into" a friend I hadn't seen in quite awhile who had been on my heart in prayer the day before. When I finished, I left the kids with the question, "So, were these coincidences or God-incidences?"

In a few short weeks the kids were coming to class with God-incidences of their own. I loved it when they said, "It was God; I know it was God!" One student couldn't even wait until class started. He came through the door, saying, "Miss Jill, it happened this week. I left my baseball stuff by the bus stop at school the other day. When it was time for practice, I couldn't find it anywhere. I thought I must have left it at home. I was going over to tell Coach, knowing I was going to be in big trouble, when my brother walked in the locker room with my stuff. He graduated last year, but just *happened* to come by the school to see his coach. He recognized my stuff, which had been out there all day, and he brought it to me 'cause otherwise he knew I'd be running laps all afternoon!"

"Did you thank your brother?" I asked.

"I did . . . but I thanked God first."

This little boy got it! He understood that serendipities are often God-ordained moments. Parents, you can help your kids see God's hand in the world by:

1. *Teaching them to say "thank you" to God first.*

   • Your son is rollerblading down a hill, gaining speed, when he realizes he's lost control and headed for the rocks at the bottom. Rather than landing in the rocks, he rolls to safety in a grassy patch. When you rush to his aide, ask him to join you in saying a "thank you" prayer to God for his protection.

   • Your teenager decides to leave a party early when a friend needs a ride, only to discover the next morning that minutes after leaving, a group of older kids showed up at the party with alcohol. Ask your teen if she believes God protected her from a dangerous situation.

2. *Helping them realize that miracles sometimes come in small packages, not just gargantuan events.*

   • Tell your children the story of Noah and the flood (Genesis 6:9–9:17). Point out that we can see big and small miracles in God's creation, for example, the gargantuan event of the flood and the quiet miracle of a rainbow. "Whenever the rainbow appears in the clouds, I will see it and remember the everlasting covenant between God and all living creatures of every kind of the earth. . . . This is the sign of the covenant I have established between me and all life on the earth." (Genesis 9:16)

- Help older children recognize the small miracles in their lives, such as when they go to youth group with a struggle in their hearts, only to have their leader talk about the issue they're dealing with.

3. *Teaching them about God's sovereignty in the world.*

- If you live in the city, make a trip to the country as often as possible. If that's not possible, visit a nearby park. Sit with your children and point out the different sounds: birds singing, crickets chirping, the wind blowing through the trees. Look at the clouds in the sky. When it snows, catch snowflakes on your tongue. When it rains, let the kids get wet. Get your children out of the house and into God's creation. Help them see that the perfect symmetry of a butterfly is absolute proof of God, the Creator.

- One of my favorite books of the Bible is Job, which teaches us much about God's sovereignty. From the monologues of Job's friends to God's dialogue with Job, we see God's reign over the earth. Job concluded, "Ask the animals, and they will teach you, or the birds of the air, and they will tell you. . . . In his hand is the life of every creature and the breath of all mankind" (Job 12:7, 10).

As your children form the holy habit of listening to God's voice and watching for his hand in their lives, they will begin to see who they really are. Paul explained it well in his letter to the Ephesians, "For we are God's workmanship, created in Christ Jesus to do good works, which God prepared in advance for us to do" (2:10). The more clearly your children see God, the more clearly they can see themselves as his servants in the world.

That was certainly true for Jennifer Hudson. Two years after her ejection from *American Idol,* she was given a prominent role in the movie *Dreamgirls.* When the Oscar nominations were given out she threw a "praise party" instead of the wild celebrations other nominees hosted. "I'm not a partier," she told reporters. "I don't drink. I don't do drugs. I'm having a praise party. The purpose of this is to praise God because he did it; I didn't." [4]

Jennifer's God-confidence enabled her to accept rejection and keep going. Her aim is to glorify God in all that she does, win or lose. She wants everyone to know that her talent has come from the Lord and that any accolades she receives belong to Him.

GIVE THEM OPPORTUNITIES TO SERVE GOD BY SERVING OTHERS

Truett Cathy has an open-door policy at his office. Families, friends, and not-yet-friends stream in and out of his office at Chick-Fil-A headquaters daily. Mr. Cathy's attitude and energy disguise that he's in his eighties. As the founder and CEO of one of America's most successful companies, he has a highly developed God-confidence that has served him well. He says, "Nearly every moment of every day we have the opportunity to give something to someone else—our time, our love, our resources. I have always found more joy in giving when I did not expect anything in return." [5]

We live in a changing world, but we need to
be reminded that the important
things have not changed, and the
important things will not change
if we keep our priorities in proper order.
TRUETT CATHY, FOUNDER OF CHICK-FIL-A

A strong Christian, Truett Cathy serves others because of his heart for God and because he has discovered the joy of helping others. You can help your children do the same. No matter your children's age, you can open doors for them to serve God and others.

My friends the Dawsons did this with their four children, and they have matured into young people with one eye on heaven and the other on earth. I asked the Dawsons what they did to cultivate a servant's heart in their kids, and have included their ideas along with my own.

Preschool through Elementary School

- Volunteer as a family to sort clothes for the local Pregnancy Care Center in your town.

- Make cards for the elderly in your church and then deliver the cards.

- Sponsor a child through a mission organization or charity, such as the Christian Children's Fund, and pray for that child and talk about that child with your children. Encourage your children to correspond with the child, asking for prayer requests.

- Encourage your child to play sports on a team. Working on a team teaches children they have responsibilities to others. If they don't do their part, the team suffers.

- Visit or call someone who can't leave home. Shut-ins love to hear the voice of a child calling just to cheer them up.

Older Elementary and Middle School

- Encourage your children to volunteer to help with a ministry associated with your church. The Dawsons' daughter volunteered weekly in retirement apartments. She visited residents and helped the administrator with office tasks. At Christmas their older children accompanied the Dawsons as they delivered Angel Tree gifts to families.

- Buy gifts for a needy family and deliver them secretly in the night so your work will be anonymous. (Your kids will love having this secret!)

- Cat-sit or dog-sit for a neighbor's pet.

- Encourage your children to spend time with the elderly— grandparents, neighbors, nursing home residents. God's Word instructs us: "Rise in the presence of the aged, show respect for the elderly and revere your God. I am the Lord" (Leviticus 19:32).

- Keep encouraging your children to play sports on a team.

- Bake cookies or an after-school snack for the children of a single parent.

High School

- Encourage teens to get a job in the service field of employment, such as at a restaurant, hotel, coffee shop, car wash, or catering business. My sons worked for a caterer through college, and the experience cultivated humility in them.

- Volunteer as a family to lead worship and to share your faith at a local retirement center.

- Encourage teens to volunteer with an organization that helps the underprivileged. For example, the Dawsons' kids participated in a biweekly after-school program for at-risk children in a nearby elementary school. They led games, helped with snacks, and interacted with the children. Their older teens were also able to help out with Habitat for Humanity during their all-church building blitz when church members worked around the clock for two weeks to build a home.

- Expect teens to help with driving responsibilities for younger siblings.

- Provide a ride for an appointment for an elderly neighbor or relative.

- Keep encouraging participation in sports or some kind of extracurricular group activity.

Children who serve others as a way of serving God will grow up to become others-centered adults. Serving others tends to demolish the selfishness in us. I'm reminded of Dr. Seuss's story about the Grinch—that fellow with the tiny heart who was green with envy. He was so selfish he wanted no one to be happy, especially the precious Whos in Whoville.

But remember the picture of the Grinch standing atop Mount Crumpit, ready to dump all the gifts he had stolen from the Whos? As he leaned over to revel in the sounds of crying and sadness, the sounds of singing and laughter filtered to the mountaintop instead. And then the most amazing thing happened. His heart began to swell to three times its size, bulging from his chest. With not a second to spare, the Grinch and his pooch, Max, tipped the sleigh away from the edge and flew down the summit back to Whoville to return all the gifts.

WHAT TEENS LEARN
FROM SERVING OTHERS

Independent Sector, an organization that studies non-profit groups, surveyed teenagers who volunteer to help others. The young people said through their service experience they:

1. Learned to respect others.

2. Gained satisfaction from helping others.

3. Learned to be helpful and kind.

4. Learned how to get along with and relate to others.

5. Learned new skills.

6. Learned to understand people who are different from them.

7. Learned how to relate to younger children.

8. Developed leadership skills.

9. Became better people.

10. Became more patient.

By giving their time and energy, many said they received more in return.[6]

Do you remember the very end of the story? The big-hearted Grinch joined in the celebration! Children find joy in serving others.

And if you've nurtured God-confidence in them, they'll gain humble confidence. Humble confidence is a by-product of God-confidence. It's the kind of confidence that doesn't take pride in the accomplishments of self, but in the knowledge of a job done well as an act of worship to God.

TEACH THEM THEIR GIFTS COME FROM GOD FOR A PURPOSE

John Ruskin said, "I believe the first test of a truly great man is his humility. I do not mean by humility, doubt of his own power, or hesitation in speaking his opinion. But really great men have a feeling that the greatness is not in them but through them; that they could not do or be anything else than God made them."[7] I agree. God created your children to "do good works," to bring glory to Him and joy to their own hearts.

My daddy was a jigsaw puzzle fanatic and he spent hours working on complex puzzles with intricate designs. He had a methodical way of going about his hobby—grouping different colors and textures together and then working on individual sections before moving them into the whole puzzle. We do the same thing with each other, don't we? We subdivide ourselves—from human beings to different nationalities, races, and socioeconomic groups, and yet, just like the pieces in Daddy's puzzle, we all have only one place to fit into God's grand puzzle.

You can begin to help your kids understand that God has a purpose for their lives, using a jigsaw puzzle as an illustration. As your children move from the wooden puzzles of farm animals to the more complex puzzles of barnyard scenes, from ten pieces to twenty-five to sixty pieces, they're ready to understand what it means to find their purpose. Sit down with them, spread a jigsaw puzzle before you, and offer this explanation:

> Look at our puzzle. We're putting the straight edges in place to give us a border to work inside, just as God gives us boundaries to live in. Each piece must be put in its correct place before another piece can be connected. The same is true with us, as we each find our place or purpose within God's plan; we help someone else find theirs. If we don't find the place carved just for us, we make it difficult for someone else to find theirs.

One of my duties before God is to help you find your purpose, your place in God's plan. He created you to fit into a special place designed for you. Here's what we're going to do:

- Read God's Word every day.

- Pray and ask God to show us His plan for you.

- Look for His signposts leading us in the right direction.

- Listen for His answers.

The first place we're going to start is in Romans 12:

> Do not conform any longer to the pattern of this world, but be transformed by the renewing of your mind. Then you will be able to test and approve what God's will is—his good, pleasing and perfect will. For by the grace given me I say to every one of you: Do not think of yourself more highly than you ought, but rather think of yourself with sober judgment, in accordance with the measure of faith God has given you. Just as each of us has one body with many members, and these members do not all have the same function, so in Christ we who are many form one body, and each

member belongs to all the others. We have different
gifts, according to the grace given us. (2–5)

You see, just like jigsaw pieces, we come in different shapes
and sizes with different abilities, but all belonging to the same
puzzle, God's grand puzzle.

Eric Liddell, the gifted athlete who ran for Scotland in the 1924 Olym-
pics, knew that God had given him an extraordinary gift for a purpose.
He found his place in God's puzzle.

Everything about him was different. He shook the hands of his
opponents and offered warm regards before every race. When the gun
sounded, he lifted his head and ran with knees rising to his chest.
While the other runners looked ahead, he looked up. Eric ran as if no one
was in the stands.

He didn't run to be seen by spectators, but by God.

Harold Abrahams, on the other hand, wasn't running *to* anything
but *from* something. Harold was running from his feelings of insecurity and doubt. He was hoping that by achieving his goal of winning a
gold medal, he would prove he was somebody. He thought achievement would bring the contentment he was missing.

During the Olympic trials Harold lost the first race of his career to
none other than Eric Liddell. Devastated, he proclaimed, "I don't run
to take a beating, I run to win. If I can't win, I won't run" to which a
friend replied, "If you don't run, you can't win." [8]

Harold was an accomplished young man. Outstanding student,
Olympic runner, but he ran for himself, not for God. His life was all
about him. He couldn't handle defeat, and he couldn't enjoy victory.
Selfishness keeps one from knowing satisfaction. Harold did go on to
win a gold medal, but he didn't find any joy in the winning. Rather
than exhilaration, he felt sadness, because he had been running for the
wrong reasons.

One young man ran for God, the other for himself. Through these two young men we can see the stark difference between confidence in God and confidence in self. One found pleasure and contentment in going beyond the Olympic track to serving God and others as a missionary in China. The other found only loss of respect and emptiness. He said he was "running but not knowing what I'm chasing."[9]

When Eric's sister expressed concern that he had lost himself in the fame, he responded, "God made me for a purpose. And he made me fast. When I run, I feel God's pleasure."[10] For Eric Liddell, running was an expression of his devotion to God's purpose in his life. He knew that God had made him fast for a reason—to run. Because he ran to please God, when he ran, he felt God's pleasure.

What a great picture of God-confidence!

CHAPTER 7

Develop a Passion for Compassion

ALEXIS, ROMI, AND Marni Barta were spring cleaning when they started talking about what to do with the large number of children's videos they had outgrown and no longer watched. One of them remembered that a young friend being treated for leukemia had spent many hours in the hospital watching movies to help distract her and pass the time. As they talked, they decided to donate the videos to the pediatric oncology center where their friend had been treated.

The hospital staff told the sisters that videos are the first thing kids ask for when they are in the hospital. In fact, the hospital greeted the donation with such enthusiasm that Alexis, Romi, and Marni decided to collect as many videos and DVDs as they could for the pediatrics departments in other hospitals—and Kids Flicks was born.

The sisters began writing solicitation letters to family, friends, and movie studios, requesting movie donations. They also started annual collection drives at all their former schools and through their pediatrician's office. They now spend many hours every week receiving and picking up donations, sorting the movies, and driving to the hospitals to drop off the donated movies. They've even begun shipping movies to hospitals in other cities, due to the overwhelming response to their requests.

To date, Kids Flicks had donated thirty-six hundred new and used movies to thirty-six different hospitals throughout the western United States. Each hospital received a movie library of one hundred assorted films. Their goal is to donate videos and DVDs to hospitals all over the country.[1]

The Barta sisters are living out Jesus's command to love your neighbor as yourself (see Mark 12:31). Not only did they forget themselves and see the needs of those around them, but they are also doing something to meet those needs. They are coming alongside those who suffer. They are getting involved and helping thousands of children who are going through a very difficult and scary experience.

They have a passion for compassion.

Merriam-Webster's defines *compassion* as "sympathetic consciousness of others' distress together with a desire to alleviate it." Compassion is stepping into the other person's shoes to make things better. Sympathizing isn't enough. Compassion is active, not passive. Sympathy + Action = Compassion. Compassion is caring so much that you do something to alleviate the other person's pain.

How can parents instill compassion in their children? It's easier said than done, isn't it? We want our children to be kind toward others. We want them to be compassionate, unselfish givers. We want them to love others without reserve. And yet, too often we see displays of utter selfishness and thoughtlessness in today's kids.

What, then, can we do to cultivate compassion in our children? Fill their hearts with love.

FILL YOUR CHILDREN WITH COMPASSIONATE LOVE

After a cancer diagnosis, major-league baseball player Brett Butler experienced the true meaning of compassion from his daughter. She came up to him after she was told her dad had cancer and said, "Daddy, I prayed to Jesus that he would give me your cancer."

Brett asked, "What did you do that for?"

She replied, "Because, Daddy, I can handle the pain better than watching you in pain."[2]

Brett's daughter would rather suffer for her father than watch him suffer. How can she possess such compassion and love? Because of the compassionate love of her father. Children love as they have been loved. If kids have been loved compassionately, that's how they love.

Compassion begins at home—as they receive love. Parents, the most important thing you can do to cultivate compassion in your children is to show them compassionate love. Make sure your kids know that you love them, fully and completely. We'll talk more about ways to do this in the next chapter, but for now let me encourage you to pray blessings over your children.

The blessing can be as simple as a prayer at bedtime or as they leave for school or sit down for dinner. Words are powerful. They can build or tear down. They can strengthen or weaken. They can bless or curse. They can fill hearts or empty hearts. God's Word spoken to our children is a powerful life changer. I started this practice when my sons were little boys and I have continued it to this day. Some of the blessings I prayed over my sons to assure them of my love were:

- "For this reason I kneel before the Father, from whom his whole family in heaven and on earth derives its name. I pray that out of his glorious riches he may strengthen you with power through his Spirit in your inner being, so that Christ may dwell in your hearts through faith. And I pray that you, being rooted and established in love, may have power, together with all the saints, to grasp how wide and long and high and deep is the love of Christ, and to know this love that surpasses knowledge—that you may be filled to the measure of all the fullness of God." (1 Ephesians 3:14–19)

- "Since the day you were born, I have not stopped praying for you and asking God to fill you with the knowledge of his will through all spiritual wisdom and understanding. And I pray this in order that you may live a life worthy of the Lord and may please him in every way; bearing fruit in every good work, growing in the knowledge of God, being strengthened with all power according to his glorious might so that you may have great endurance and patience, and joyfully giving thanks to the Father, who has qualified you to share in the inheritance of the saints in the kingdom of light." (Colossians 1:9–12, author's paraphrase)

- "May our Lord Jesus Christ himself and God our Father, who loved us and by his grace gave us eternal encouragement and good hope, encourage your hearts and strengthen you in every good deed and word." (2 Thessalonians 2:16–17)

Not only can you fill your kids up with your love, you can also fill them with assurances of God's love. Make sure they know that God loves them, fully and completely. Take them to the window and help them see Him looking back at them in love. When our children accept God's love and love Him in return, they will freely offer love and compassion to others.

This was true for the child of a friend of mine. Her husband had left her and their son when he was an infant. This precious child grew up never knowing his earthly father, but his mother saturated him with her love and God's Word. Her son is now a grown man, serving God in full-time ministry. He has an intimate relationship with God

BLESSINGS FOR YOUR CHILDREN

Blessings are abundant in Scripture.
You could pray a different blessing from Scripture
every week for more than a year and
still not run out.
Let me get you started:

Numbers 6:23–26
Deuteronomy 6
Deuteronomy 28:3–6
Psalm 1
Psalm 15
Psalm 20:1–2, 4–5
Psalm 112:1–3, 4, 6
Psalm 121:5–8
Proverbs 2:1–8
Proverbs 3:1–4
Proverbs 3:5–8
Romans 15:5–6, 13, 33
1 Thessalonians 5:23–24, 28
2 Thessalonians 2:16–17, 3:16
Hebrews 13:21–22

because God has been his only father since birth. His understanding of God's love surpasses those of us twice his age.

Love for God and love for others go hand in hand.

Parents, it is our holy duty and sacred honor as Christian parents to show our children the love of God through our actions and words.

When we love our children with the love we have received from God, they will respond to His love. They will understand how it feels to be loved unconditionally and will want to love others in return.

Max Lucado offers his insight into the order of receiving and giving love:

> Could it be that the first step of love is not toward them but toward him? Could it be that the secret to loving is receiving? You give love by first receiving. "We love each other as a result of his loving us first" (1 John 4:19 NLT). If we haven't received these things ourselves, how can we give them to others? Apart from God, "the heart is deceitful above all things" (John 17:9). We need help from an outside source. A transfusion. Would we love as God loves? Then we start by receiving God's love.[3]

Compassionate living is receiving God's love and loving others as we have been loved. Compassionate living is doing something to help those in need—whether that's the members of your family, your next-door neighbor, or a stranger.

Jesus said, "A new command I give you: Love one another. As I have loved you, so you must love one another. By this all men will know that you are my disciples, if you love one another" (John 13:34–35). We offer compassion to others as a way of showing Who we belong to, as a way of showing others the love that's available to them through Christ.

Your children receive their first lessons in compassion from watching you.

MODEL COMPASSION

Your children want to be proud of you. They want to have parents they can brag about. Their identity is so wrapped up in yours, they gain confidence in themselves by having confidence in you. They want to be just like you, so they want and need you to be the person they would like to become.

If you want to raise compassionate children, let your kids catch you doing compassionate acts like the following:

- Offer a helpful hand to your spouse when he or she is overwhelmed with a commitment.

- Take your kids to visit someone who lives alone.

- Write a letter of encouragement to someone.

- Read the Bible to someone too ill to read.

- Invite a nonbeliever to do a Bible study with you.

- Show compassion to your kids:

  - Take a deep breath before you blow up when your ten-year-old accidentally steps on your favorite fishing rod.

  - The next time your teenager says he was in the wrong place at the wrong time and needs your help, remember what it was like to be sixteen, and offer a hug and constructive help rather than a tongue lashing.

  - Clean your daughter's room for her because you know she's had a hard day at school.

  - When your six-year-old has a meltdown because of exhaustion, pick up your child and read a book instead of losing patience. Afterward you can dole out the appropriate discipline.

However, the most powerful way you can model compassion is to show compassion to yourself. When we can accept our own weaknesses and limits, we are better able to accept the weaknesses and limits of others.

Locked your keys in the car? Most of us are trained to react by berating our own stupidity or bewailing our fate. Instead, be compassionate with yourself. Let your children hear you say, "Wow, I must really be distracted." This will help them realize that we all do the best we can, and sometimes our best is not so good, but that's okay. When your kids see you showing compassion to yourself, it gives them permission to treat their own mistakes with compassion, and by extension, have compassion for others.

It's also important that you be honest about how difficult it is sometimes to be compassionate. When you're in a hurry, and the checker takes forever, have the courage to say to your child, "I'm in such a hurry, it's hard to be compassionate and realize she is working as fast as she can."

Not only do we need to model compassion, if we want to raise compassionate kids, we also need to teach empathy and understanding.

TEACH EMPATHY AND UNDERSTANDING

One hot and humid August afternoon the boys and I stopped at the dry cleaners to pick up an order. Dorothy, the woman behind the counter, looked whipped. She tried to keep a pleasant countenance, but we could tell she was exhausted.

I commented on the heat and asked if she was okay. Her response, "Did you know in the winter we don't need heat 'cause the cleaning machines produce enough? In the summer if it's a hundred degrees outside, it's a hundred and twenty degrees in here with those machines. But I guess I'm okay. We keep the back doors open to keep the air moving." Another woman appeared from the steam room looking more hot and tired than Dorothy.

I kept thinking about those women as we left the parking lot. I looked at the boys, "Guys, we've gotta' help them," and drove straight to a grocery store. The boys grabbed a Styrofoam chest and filled it with ice while I picked up bottled water, sports drinks, and snack food. We headed back to the laundry. Can you imagine the look on those women's faces when we walked in?

Dorothy hollered, "Y'all come see," to the women in the back. The boys beamed as they handed out drinks and offered snacks. "God loves you and we do, too," we said, while the workers enjoyed a respite from the heat.

My sons haven't forgotten that day. They learned a lesson in empathy, "the action of understanding, being aware of, being sensitive to, and vicariously experiencing the feelings, thoughts, and experience of another." Their minds saw people working hard in difficult conditions, but their hearts understood that these women needed a bit of encouragement.

As our children develop empathy, they become connected to the people around them, not just their friends, and their self-centeredness gives way to others-centeredness. They see the world with the eyes of their hearts. They see the needs of others.

Part of teaching empathy means promoting understanding. When you point out to your kids the reasons another person is acting "weird" (as kids will say) or in an unusual manner, you are helping your children understand that person's actions, which can lead to empathy rather than ridicule.

Dr. Ellen Iscoe,[4] a psychologist in Washington, D.C., who works with parents and children, offers this example:

Ten-year-old Brenda comes home from school and announces huffily, "I just hate Megan. She thinks she is sooo smart. Anytime the teacher asks us anything, she just starts talking and talking like she is the only one who knows!" Her mother does not need to dispute the classmate is annoying. That empathizes with Brenda's annoyance and demonstrates acceptance of her feelings. But how much more powerful is the intervention if her mother continues with the statement: "Did you know some people's brains work differently from yours? There are some people who just need to think out loud. Maybe Megan's just thinking when she talks in class and not showing off." By adding this statement, you teach your child not to rush to judgment and to consider that there might be other factors beyond what she sees and observes.[5]

With that said, here are some ways you can help your children develop empathy and understanding through every stage of their growing-up years:

Tots to Tykes (From Two Years Old to Six Years Old)

- Offer sympathy when your children get hurt. This helps them experience how it feels to receive empathy and teaches them to empathize with the hurts of other children.

- Say a prayer with your children the next time you hear a siren or see an emergency situation. Talk with them about what that siren means and why someone might need their prayers. Show them how to think outside themselves by praying for others in need.

- When your children take a toy away from another child who gets upset, ask your children how they would feel if someone took away their toy. Teaching your children to put themselves in the other person's place is the beginning of developing empathy. Teach your child the Golden Rule: treat others the way you want to be treated.

Tweens (From Six Years Old to Twelve Years Old)

- Read *Charlotte's Web* and point out Charlotte's amazing un-selfish devotion to Wilbur in keeping her promise. Wilbur's persistence to help "the rat" become a better rat is a great example of putting yourself in another's shoes. Wilbur understood why the rat was so cantankerous and wanted to help him "get over himself," so he could become one of the "gang."

- Teach tweens how to show understanding toward the elderly by offering Grandma or Grandpa their seat, walking slowly with them through the mall, and visiting great-grandparents in nursing homes. This helps your children understand how difficult growing older can be.

- Have your tweens help you make a special treat for a stressed-out older sibling or parent. Explain that this service is not about them, but about showing empathy and understanding toward a loved one in need.

Teens (From Thirteen Years Old to Nineteen Years Old)

- Listen empathically when your teens are frustrated, angry, overwhelmed, or sad. Keep in mind that teenagers need more listening than they need problem-solving. They need to know you care enough to let them vent. For instance, when your daughter comes in the back door, exhausted from overcommitment and angry at the world, she doesn't need you to tell her she needs to drop one of her activities or get more rest, she needs you to be an empathetic listener. She'll probably solve her problem in the process of venting, then give you credit for "always being there to listen"!

- Ask "How would you feel if . . ." when your teen makes an unkind remark about another person. I know one mom who overheard her son, Walt, making fun of a custodian with limited mental abilities. She asked her son, "How would you feel if you were born with the same limitations that Mr. William has?" Not only did she expect an answer, she asked Walt to write down his answers and take time to think about it. This wise mom showed her son how to put himself in another's shoes. A couple of weeks later, Walt befriended the custodian by offering to take him to a minor-league baseball game. As her son and Mr. William got to know each other, Walt discovered that Mr. William was quite an expert in history. You guessed it. Mr. William helped Walt with memorizing all those historical facts and dates.

From tykes to teens, our children can develop empathy. They can learn to look at situations from another's viewpoint. The next time your kids fight with each other, look at it as an opportunity to teach them a lesson in extending compassion. Ask them to each retrieve a pair of shoes, and then exchange those shoes with each other for a day (not to wear, but as a reminder), instructing them to look at the dispute from the other person's point of view. (You can do this with kids of any age. It wouldn't hurt to do this with your spouse occasionally!)

Here's the clincher. Before your children return each other's shoes, read the story of Jesus washing His disciples' feet (John 13). Then have your children clean their brother's or sister's shoes before returning them.

The act of cleaning another person's shoes, especially your sibling's, is a heart-changing experience. Couple it with the telling of Jesus washing the disciples' feet, and parents have a powerful teaching moment.

I'm often asked if my boys have always been close. The obvious answer is yes, by virtue of being twins, having the same friends and interests. But the whole truth and nothing but the truth is they have had their knock-down, drag-out fights. They've had seasons, short-lived, but still seasons when they were just sick of each other. During their tyke years, I could require a kiss and a hug to make up their spats. But not in their tween years. When nothing I could do or say would help take the edge off their edginess, I'd suggest that they "walk in your brother's shoes," and often it would do the trick!

Helping our children develop empathy and understanding also means teaching them how to love as Jesus tells us to love.

TEACH YOUR CHILDREN HOW TO LOVE OTHERS

Most Christians are familiar with 1 Corinthians 13, the "love chapter." But the inherent danger with such familiar passages of Scripture is that we become desensitized to what they mean and what actions they urge us to take. One way to make this passage come alive is to insert your name into verses 4–7:

> [Jill] is patient, [Jill] is kind. [Jill] does not envy, [Jill] does not boast, [Jill] is not proud. [Jill] is not rude, [Jill] is not self-seeking, [Jill] is not easily angered, [Jill] keeps no record of wrongs. [Jill] does not delight in evil but rejoices with the truth. [Jill] always protects, always trusts, always hopes, always perseveres.

When you insert your name in the passage, you'll probably feel as motivated (and uncomfortable) as I feel right now. I'm certainly not all these things, but this exercise gives me a clear picture of what real love is—and what I need to work toward to become an empathetic giver.

Now, do this exercise with your children. If they are too young to read, read the passage aloud for them. What a beautiful affirmation for young children to hear from a parent. As soon as the children are able, have them read it on their own as a reminder of who they can become in Christ.

Now let's look at another way to promote empathy and understanding.

> Jesus said, "Whoever receives this
> little child in my name receives me;
> and whoever receives me receives him who sent me.
> For he who is least among you all will be great."
> LUKE 9:48 NKJV

PRACTICE HOSPITALITY

Scripture doesn't suggest that Christians be hospitable. It commands us to be. Even though some folks are naturally more outgoing than others, hospitality can be learned by all.

The word *hospitality* comes from the Greek word *philonexia*, which means, "To entertain strangers, love of strangers."[6] Throughout the New Testament, we're told to offer *philonexia* (hospitality):

> Share with God's people who are in need. Practice hospitality.
>
> ROMANS 12:13

> Offer hospitality to one another without grumbling.
>
> 1 PETER 4:9

> We ought therefore to show hospitality to such men
> so that we may work together for the truth.
>
> 3 JOHN 1:8

I know of no better example of hospitality than the Howard family. Chrys and John Howard have had someone live with them for most of their thirty-six years of marriage. They have "moved over" for family or friends who need a place to stay while they built a new house, moved to the area, or regrouped. They've also had foster children, unwed mothers, missionaries, and an exchange student. In total they have had seventy houseguests who have stayed for more than a month, and some of those have stayed more than a year. That number doesn't even include all the youth group kids, traveling singing groups, and family visitors from out of town.

The Howards never apologized to their children for asking them to give up their beds or rearrange for someone else. They just presented it as a fun adventure and a way to get to know someone new. It was part of sharing with others what they had been given. Consequently when their kids had shared their room for weeks, they accepted it as part of their family's mission.

When I asked Chrys how this had benefited her children, she told me:

> John and I are blessed to have parents who opened their homes in the same way when we were growing up. We both learned the importance of hospitality from our parents and hope that we have passed that gift on to our children.
>
> Being hospitable involves all the Fruits of the Spirit— patience, kindness, love, joy, and more. I know our children were able to see those, not just in us, but in our many guests. Each visitor brought us something special—not material gifts, but eternal gifts. I admit, some guests were challenging to have in our home, but we learned life lessons, and the stories are now a part of our family history that makes us laugh as we retell some interesting events.

Now, most of us don't have the room or the pocketbooks to accommodate an unending stream of guests, but we can certainly learn a lot about sharing our home from the Howard family.

1. Our homes don't belong to us. They belong to God. If we have a roof over our heads, we have more than a lot of folks. We should be willing to open our homes when needed.

2. There's no need to treat your guests like company, treat them like family. You don't need to change the sheets every day or prepare gourmet meals.

3. Children can learn important life lessons when they have the opportunity to interact with different personalities and temperaments.

4. The lack of a guest room isn't a reason for not having houseguests. A few times a year I visit dear friends whose daughters take turns being bumped from their beds. Their home is always open for whoever needs a place to lay their head—even on a moment's notice.

But having houseguests isn't the only way to practice hospitality. Here are other ideas you might want to adopt:

- Offer your home as a shelter from life's storms. Invite folks for dinner who are in need of a listening ear—an elderly neighbor or someone who has recently suffered a divorce or the loss of a loved one.

- Offer to baby-sit for a young couple one Saturday afternoon at your house to give them the opportunity to take care of household chores that are difficult when they have a new baby or young children at home.

- Share hospitality outside your home by taking "dinner in a bag" to a shut-in. Prepare the meal in their home. Many elderly people enjoyed the hustle and bustle that used to be in their homes. The silence becomes deafening as the days pass by and their home remains still. Most folks enjoy the sounds of cooking in their kitchen and the sweet aroma of a pie baking in the oven. They appreciate the company even more than the hot meal.

- Offer your home to your children's youth group, missionaries, or people in town for funerals, weddings, or medical emergencies with family members.

- Open your home to celebrate the special events in your friends' and family's lives, such as baby or wedding showers, birthday celebrations, promotions, and so on. Don't panic—these are all events that others can pitch in to help with the arrangements.

If you're intimidated by the prospect of having people in your home, I want to encourage you not to be. It's not the size or décor of a home that makes it special, but the love that fills it. Hospitality isn't just entertaining others, it's loving others. And it's the love that's much more important.

> Dear children,
> let us not love with words or tongue
> but with actions and in truth.
> 1 JOHN 3:18

One final way you can help your kids grow up to become empathetic adults is by involving them in acts of compassion.

Involve Your Children in Acts of Compassion

Wesley Willis, vice president of Fort Wayne Bible College, tells this story of a friend who lives a compassionate life and taught his reluctant teenager the richness of serving without compensation.

Mr. Willis's friend, a professor, supplemented his salary by painting houses during the summer. His next-door neighbor was impressed with this and decided to paint his own house. But it was a new experience for the neighbor, and progress was painfully slow. One Saturday, when the neighbor was out of town, Mr. Willis's friend called his teenage son aside and suggested that they do some painting for the neighbor. The son asked what they would charge for the painting. When his father said there would be no charge—they would do it as neighbors—the young man was incredulous.

That Saturday father and son team-painted one side of the house, which was more than the neighbor would have accomplished in a week. When he arrived home, he was overwhelmed by this expression of love by an acquaintance.

TWELVE THINGS TO DO TODAY (AND EVERY DAY)

1. Open a door for someone and allow him or her to go through first.

2. Smile and say "Good morning" to those you meet.

3. Say "Thank you" for small courtesies.

4. Compliment someone for a job well done.

5. Return the shopping cart to its holding bin before leaving the parking lot.

6. Send a thank-you note to a public official.

7. Do something kind for someone anonymously.

8. Keep fast-food certificates in the car to give to folks asking for help.

9. Add "God bless you" to your good-byes.

10. Pick up trash on the sidewalks.

11. Put coins in a meter that's expired.

12. Learn the name and one fact about the folks you see every day, but haven't taken the time to get to know.

At the day's end, when the neighbor expressed his gratitude, Mr. Willis's son said to his father, "That was really neat. When can we do it again?" Not only had the father demonstrated compassion by helping out a neighbor, he also gave his son a vision for reaching out to others. This father helped his son discover one of the greatest joys on earth . . . giving without expectation of return. And the son wanted more of it.[7]

If you involve your children in acts of compassion, they will be far more likely to open their hearts to others-centeredness. Are you ready to sign your family up to serve? Let me offer a few suggestions.

Tots to Tykes (From Two Years Old to Six Years Old)

- Encourage your children to show concern for others. For example, give them a few pennies to share whenever a person asks for money. Drop a coin in the box at McDonald's. Buy an extra canned good for the food barrel. Be sure to explain who you are giving the money to and why.

- Help your kids learn to watch for ways to be of service by saying, "Look, someone needs your help," when you notice an elderly person who needs his or her car door opened or a child alone on the playground who needs a friend. Point out to your children that they are "appointed" at that moment to help someone in need.

- Teach your children to give 10 percent of their allowance to the church offering. Explain that the offering we give enables the church to fulfill its mission from God to take care of those in need.

- Help tykes sort through their toys once a year and give them to a local charity. Encourage your kids to personally give one of their toys to a child in need.

Tweens (From Six Years Old to Twelve Years Old)

- Encourage your tweens to collect homework and textbooks for a sick classmate and take them to the classmate after school.

- Your tweens can become good listeners, which is a character trait of a compassionate person. Ask your kids how their friends are doing. Remind your tweens to make time to talk to their friends about their struggles. Remind them to ask, "What's wrong?" if they notice a friend in a bad mood or with a sudden mood change.

- Help your tweens form the habit of calling grandparents on a regular basis if they live out of town. Remind them how much it means to your parents to talk to their grandkids.

- Not every tween is meant to play on the football team, but your child needs to participate in organized sports, musical competitions, or some kind of team activity. Too many kids today are allowed to sequester themselves in their rooms with their boxes . . . from iPods to PCs to big-screen televisions. Please hear me when I say that's simply unacceptable. *The more time a child spends alone, the more self-focused he or she becomes.*

Teens (From Thirteen Years Old to Nineteen Years Old)

- Encourage your teens to baby-sit, teach Sunday school, work at summer camp or Vacation Bible School, teach swim lessons, and so on. Your teens need to experience working in a job that serves others, whether or not they get paid. They can work for money to learn responsibility, but working for free in order to meet another's need develops compassion.

- Encourage your teens to become readers at a local elementary school. All it takes is thirty minutes once a week to change a child's life. Remind your teens that they're already leaders—younger kids are watching and emulating their behavior.

- Encourage your teens to befriend the new kids in school by inviting them home after school or to school events. Remind teens how uncomfortable it is to be the "new kid on the block."

- Continue to encourage participation in a team activity. The surest way to keep your teens from developing compassion is to allow them to become isolated. If your son or daughter prefers being alone to participating in extracurricular activities, encourage him or her to get out. (I understand there can be medical reasons, but apart from medical reasons, get the kids out of their rooms! It doesn't have to be a strenuous activity, but a *group* activity.) There's truly something for everyone available today. Check out your local YMCA for a wide variety of affordable group activities.

With your help, your kids can learn to put others ahead of themselves, just as Scripture admonishes:

Therefore, as God's chosen people, holy and dearly loved, clothe yourselves with compassion, kindness, humility, gentleness and patience. Bear with each other and forgive whatever grievances you may have against one another. Forgive as the Lord forgave you. And over all these virtues put on love, which binds them all together in perfect unity. (Colossians 3:12–14)

The rewards of cultivating compassion in our kids far exceeds the effort it requires of us. My sons showered me with compassion and empathy one day when I least expected it.

DISASTER TURNED DELIGHT

"We'll take care of it, Mom," the twins proclaimed as they ran for their room the morning of their eighth birthday.

The circle in front of our home was transformed into a pirates' island to welcome twenty swashbucklers and maidens for boat races around the cul-de-sac, a treasure hunt, and of course, cake and ice cream. Everything was perfect—until I walked into the kitchen an hour before the festivities to find the birthday cake in shambles. The boys heard my cry and came running.

I had stayed up till the wee hours of the morning before to finish the most spectacular pirates' ship cake you've ever seen. (Well, maybe not the most spectacular, but for a homemade cake, it wasn't too bad.) Two round chocolate cake layers, cut in half, stood on edge to form the ship's body, held in place with icing "glue." The mainsail and the flying jib fastened to shish-kabob sticks waved in the breeze of the air conditioning. The Calico Jack was a worthy vessel ready to be devoured by hungry pirates. At least, that was the case when I went to bed.

By morning the side of the ship had collapsed. The entire middle section was in crumbles. The cake was ruined, and there was no time to start over.

When they saw my tears, my little pirates shouted, "Don't worry, Mom! We know what to do," as they ran in the kitchen with a tub of Lego blocks.

Before I could dry my eyes, the boys positioned two pirate ships with cannons aimed at the crumbled cake on either side of the cake board, and placed pirate figures all over, as if the pirates were treading water, waiting to be rescued. "Mom, look, Mom, she took a direct hit, but she didn't sink," they said in unison. "Mom, Mom, please don't be sad. This is the best cake ever—it's real. Pirates always blasted each other."

Now, think about this a minute. The boys could have "lost it" when they saw their ruined birthday cake. They could have walked away, in spite of my tears, leaving me in my sorrow. They could have made fun of me for making a mess of their cake. But they didn't. Instead, they showed great compassion.

It turned out to be a special day for all. My sons enjoyed celebrating the milestone of their eighth birthday, while I celebrated the growth I could see in their hearts. They saw my frustration and did something in order to make me feel better. The compassion that filled their hearts filled my heart with joy.

CHAPTER 8
Build Family Togetherness

W HEN I THINK of family togetherness, I think of the Cavaliers. Ferdinand and Emily have ten children, twenty-six grandchildren, thirty-six great-grandchildren, and nine great-great-grandchildren to date. They know the true meaning of family. With the exception of one brother, all of Ferdinand and Emily's children live within an hour of each other, and there haven't been any divorces in this family. They say they have too much accountability to fail.

Even when their immediate family grew to number seventy-five, anyone in town who needed a meal was welcome at Ferdinand and Emily's home. On special days, the house was filled with standing room only by ten o'clock in the morning. The family was so large they had to turn the hall into a dining space for children under twelve, and the children loved it. They called it eating "toe to toe," because they formed two lines on either side of the wide hallway with toes touching the child sitting across from them, as they ate their meal. One of the great-grandchildren told me, "No other kids I know eat on the floor but the Cavaliers. That makes our family special." When the children turned twelve and had to eat with the adults, they were unhappy about leaving the closeness and uniqueness of eating "toe to toe."

When their kids were growing up, Emily never allowed anyone in the kitchen without an invitation during the two weeks she was cooking for Christmas day. She took great pride in preparing every morsel her family consumed. She didn't shop, she cooked. No complaints from her family. Her gift was the most enjoyed of all!

Mealtime was family time. Problems were solved, disputes settled, and laughter was shared. Personal agendas were set aside when the dinner bell rang, whether it sounded at breakfast, lunch, or dinner. All ages joined each other at the table. No one was excused. What a great lesson in selflessness for children, and Mom and Dad, too. Such times of family togetherness helped instill the belief in the children that "it's not about me, it's about others."

Emily and Ferdinand modeled this, even to the point of self-sacrifice, as seen in the following story told to me by the youngest son. "During my teenage years, I worked at the only grocery store in town. Then PayLess opened a supermarket the last year I worked at the grocery. They had the buying power to undercut our little country store. When my dad insisted that the family keep buying from the small grocery, I told him I thought the decision was foolish, particularly since we didn't have excess money."

"Dad didn't hesitate to remind me of our family's values. He said, 'Son, that man you're working for used to load up his pirogue and come down the bayou to bring us poor folks food. He traded food for moss, and if we didn't have any moss, he'd give us credit till we did. If it hadn't been for him, we would have starved to death. As long as he can keep the grocery open, we'll buy from him. You don't abandon a man just because it would make your life easier.' "

This son has never forgotten the life lesson his father taught him that day.

A few years ago I spent a Valentine's Day with about forty members of this extraordinary family. Ferdinand and Emily were being honored at a press conference as Louisiana's longest-married couple. When the lights of the television cameras dimmed and the reporters finished their questioning, Emily, ninety, looked at Ferdinand, ninety-six, and said with a school-girl giggle, "Kissie, kissie." He responded with the tenderest gesture of affection I have ever witnessed, leaning forward to bring his lips to hers with a love that has lasted for seventy-six years.

This is a family who knows who they are and Who they serve, and their times together as a family reinforced those family values of selfless giving so deeply that four generations later, the Cavaliers are still serving others.

WHY IS FAMILY TOGETHERNESS IMPORTANT?

You can have a similar impact on your own children if you will make family togetherness a priority in your home. Underneath the disappointments, the moments of anger, and the stress and strain of living together, love is the thread that holds a family together. Love isn't just an emotion, it's a choice. You can choose to love when you're angry. You can choose to love when you're disappointed. You can choose to love when you don't *feel* love.

Parents, your children will love others as you have loved them. A child whose heart is filled with the love of his parents doesn't need to look in the world for his or her heart to be filled. Money and things won't fill a child's heart. Time, discipline, and words of affirmation fill a child's heart with love. You can fill your child's heart when you spend time just being together as a family, listening, talking, and working on projects.

Working together is crucial because it teaches kids to do their part for the good of the whole. If a family member doesn't carry out an assigned duty, the household can't run smoothly. If children don't do their part as a family team member, the family team can't win.

The more children participate in the family, the less they think of themselves and wanting to do their own thing because they find more pleasure in being part of the family. Rather than closing their bedroom doors to play the guitar for hours in solitary, the more likely they will be to bring the guitar to the den to share their music with the family. They want to share their pleasure in playing the guitar with others.

Even though more and more families seem to eat their meals on the run, particularly as their children get older, I want to encourage you to resist this trend. Families that eat together have frequent times of family togetherness, and these families also seem to have fewer behavioral problems.

The National Center on Addiction and Substance Abuse at Columbia University conducted a study in 2005 that demonstrates the value of eating together as family. According to their findings:

- Nearly 70 percent of teens who eat dinner with their parents five to seven times a week say that their parents are very proud of them, compared to 48 percent of teens who have family dinners two times a week or less.

- Nearly one in five teens who have family dinners two times a week or less report that there is a great deal of tension or stress at home between family members, compared to 7 percent of teens who have at least five family dinners per week.

- Teens who have frequent family dinners are likelier than those who have infrequent family dinners to say they would turn to one or both of their parents if they had a serious problem. Teens who can confide in their parents are at much lower risk for substance abuse than teens who would confide in another adult or who have no adult in whom to confide.[1]

The study also found that teens who have five or more family dinners a week have lower rates of teen smoking, drinking, and drug use. Teens who have two or less are:

- Three times likelier to try marijuana.

- Two and a half times likelier to smoke cigarettes.

- More than one and a half times likelier to drink alcohol.[2]

Topics that most teens say they discuss at the family table include: school and sports (86 percent), friends and social activities (76 percent), current events (63 percent), and family issues or problems (58 percent). Topics that most teens wish they could honestly discuss with their parents during mealtime include: religious matters (51 percent), curfews (51 percent), peer pressure (44 percent), and dating (42 percent).[3]

I am not surprised by these findings because the give and take of conversation, the helping out in the preparation and cleaning up of the meal, and the time spent together rather than apart all contribute to the development of others-centeredness. At the family dinner table, children:

- Learn to listen to others rather than just focusing on themselves.

- Develop a deep sense of empathy for the problems of others.

- Learn to appreciate rather than just tolerate the differences in others.

But family togetherness needn't be confined to the dinner table. And, in order to encourage you to create additional opportunities for

MAKING FAMILY
MEALTIMES ENJOYABLE

To make mealtime most enjoyable, Kathleen Zelman, a columnist with WebMD, offers these suggestions:

- Establish a minimum number of family meals per week that suits your lifestyle. Start slowly, and build up to a number that works with everyone's schedule.

- Be prepared. Keep ingredients for healthful meals on hand so that preparation is easy and less time-consuming.

- Keep it simple. Family meals don't need to be elaborate. Make meals that appeal to everyone in the family.

- Cook a big pot of something delicious during the weekend for easy meal prep on busy weekdays. Or try a Crock-pot dish that you put together before leaving for work in the morning, and come home to the delicious smell of a cooked meal.

- Make mealtime enjoyable so children will treasure the ritual. Leave the serious discussions and disciplinary action for some other time. Family meals are for healthy nourishment, comfort, and support.

- Share the family ritual with friends and extended family members.[4]

family togetherness, I've compiled a list of family projects that can help you enjoy each other's company each month of the year.

FAMILY TOGETHERNESS THROUGHOUT THE YEAR

January
Make a Time Capsule Together

We can get so caught up in day-to-day living that we forget to make a life for our children. It doesn't take more money, it just takes time to make memories with your family.

Rather than make resolutions with each New Year, agree to live intentionally, not accidentally. To get started, make a family time capsule as a fun project with a deeper meaning:

- Take individual photographs of each family member and also a group photo of your family.

- Let each member add a special memento of their favorite pastime.

- Ask each member to write a letter describing their friends, activities, and those things nearest and dearest to their hearts.

- Take the "vital" statistics of weight and height. (Yes, Mom and Dad, too.)

- Add a copy of the January 1 newspaper for that year.

Have your children decorate a large oatmeal cereal box to serve as your time capsule. Seal the box with packing tape and store in a safe place. When the next January rolls around, open the box together and enjoy the memories of the past year and look forward to the new year.

February
Share the Love on Valentine's Day

If you run into me on Valentine's Day, you're likely to get a hug and a kiss, whether friend or foe. Many years ago I started a tradition of keeping a sack of chocolate hugs and kisses with me on this special day of love. Yes, I'm one of those hopelessly optimistic romantics who just loves to love. My heart warms when I see the faces of delighted strangers as they accept a tiny piece of chocolate.

"Would you like a sweet treat for Valentine's Day?" I asked an elderly gentleman one day. He was so startled, all he could do was smile. I placed a few chocolate hugs and kisses in his hand and said, "God loves you." His smile widened as his eyes sparkled with joy. I wondered how long it had been since he had heard those three little words. I wondered if he had ever heard them.

Valentine's Day is an opportunity to teach your children how to spread God's love without reserve. They can experience the truth that the more love you give away, the more you have to give.

The week before the big day, gather your children and, if you're really brave, a few of their friends for a card-making party. Collect construction paper, glue sticks, buttons, bits of lace, copies of sheet music, heart stickers, and assorted paper cut-outs. Let the kids use their imaginations to make one-of-a-kind creations for family and friends they can give out on Valentine's Day.

Here are some ideas for sharing the love on Valentine's Day:

- Serve heart-shaped pancakes for breakfast.

- Fill your family's backpacks and briefcases with love notes.

- Leave a homemade Valentine with a little bit of chocolate for the postal carrier.

- Take your coworkers old-fashioned children's cards with a sweet treat.

- Surprise your friends with a card left at their door.

- Take along a bag of hugs and kisses for everyone you meet.

- After school take the kids around the neighborhood to put a new spin on "Trick or Treat." Knock on your neighbor's doors with a "Treat for a Sweet." Your kids will love sharing candy or cookies when they see the delight of your neighbors.

- Prepare a special supper of everyone's favorites foods, even if the selections don't really go together.

- Leave the television off for the evening and enjoy each other's company.

- Read an old classic book aloud before bedtime.

- Include a special time of prayer for the unloved—orphans, widows, the homeless.

- Give out real hugs and kisses with "I love you" as you tuck everyone in for the night.

Don't let Valentine's Day pass without teaching your children, "What the world needs now is love, *God's* love. No not just for some, but for everyone."

March
Grow a Garden

My precious Mamaw White once said, "All a child needs to learn about life can be taught in the garden." After retirement Mamaw and Papaw moved to a farm out in the country. Until Mamaw's dying day she donned a bonnet and a long calico dress when she worked in the garden. When my family came to her house, we'd find her gathering fresh butter beans in her apron pockets for lunch. Those fresh beans were the perfect side dish to the best fried chicken ever cooked in a black iron skillet. To guarantee an afternoon nap, Mamaw offered her indescribable chocolate pie to finish us off.

God blessed Mamaw and Papaw with a garden that provided enough produce for several families. My grandparents showed me the joy that comes from laboring in love as they shared their bounty with family, neighbors, strangers, and anyone in need. A day in the garden "digging in God's dirt" with Mamaw and Papaw taught me a strong work ethic.

Even if you don't have a big yard, or a yard at all, you can teach your kids how to give by growing! Pull up that old red wagon. Fill it with a few inches of good-quality potting soil and start planting. Use your imagination to come up with a unique container for your family's garden.

According to Ted Hullum, an ornamental horticulturist with Home Depot, your children can grow their own salad using five-gallon buckets. Drill three holes on the side of the bucket near the bottom. (Ted cautions to drill the holes on the side rather than the bottom to prevent soil from leaking out.) Add two inches of rock. Fill with potting soil. Plant an "Early Girl" or cherry tomato plant with an old mop handle for support. Plant lettuce in the center of a second bucket. Draw a circle around the lettuce two inches from the edge of container, and drop in a thin line of carrot seeds. Place the tomato in full sun and water often. Place the salad bucket in partial shade. In forty-five days you'll have a bountiful harvest with enough to share.

Let nature's new season bring a new season to your family. Vow to spend more time in the outdoors this spring. Make schedule changes that allow for digging in the dirt, watching a tomato plant grow, and teaching your children the really important stuff of life. (Check out this great website, www.kidsgardening.org, which is packed with fresh ideas.)

April
Retell the Easter Story with Your Family

Find a special place in your home—the dining table, kitchen counter, bookshelf, or living room table—to build a display that tells the Easter story. Involve the entire family. Younger children can gather the materials and build the scene, while teenagers can read the passages each day.

- Palm Sunday—Make the base using a large piece of Styrofoam covered with sheet moss. Cut palm fronds from green construction paper. Ask the children to place the fronds around the base while someone reads Luke 19:28–48.

- Monday—Borrow a donkey from your Nativity set and place it on the fronds. Read Luke 20.

- Tuesday—Add thirty nickels to the display to represent Judas's pay of silver coins. Read Luke 21.

- Wednesday—Make three crosses from twigs gathered from the yard and bound together with twine. Press the crosses into the foam. Read Luke 22.

- Thursday—Hang a small grapevine wreath on the center cross to represent the crown of thorns. Read Luke 23:44–49.

- Friday—Encourage each family member to offer prayers of gratitude for God's amazing plan of salvation. Read Luke 23:44–49.

- Saturday—Build Jesus's tomb by gluing rocks around a toilet paper roll cut in half. Place a large stone at one end. Read Luke 23:50–56.

- Easter morning—Replace the grapevine wreath with a crown. Read Luke 24.

Without Jesus there is no Christmas. Without Jesus there is no Resurrection Sunday. By the time the boys turned five I was determined to find ways to keep Jesus in the center of our celebrations. The boys left their baskets by the kitchen window in anticipation of a visit from the Easter Bunny each year. I didn't want to stop this tradition, but change the focus.

When the boys ran to the kitchen Easter morning, they found the usual chocolate bunnies and marshmallow chicks, but they also found a rustic, handmade cross sitting in a place of honor in the center of the basket of goodies. After studying the basket's contents, Boyce looked up and said, "Mom, Mom, the Easter Bunny put the cross in the middle. He wants us to know Jesus is 'more better' than He is!"

Every year since, the boys have found a cross in the middle of their Easter baskets. When they entered the teen years, I added a good book to inspire their walk with Christ. Between you and me, I can't wait to start this tradition with grandchildren!

May
Focus on Manners

What does it mean to treat a lady like a lady? Dad, give your sons a lesson in chivalry by teaching them how to care for their mother and respect their sisters. What does it mean to "act like a lady?" Mom, give your daughter a lesson in becoming a lady. You'll be giving all your children skills that will serve them well in the years ahead.

Use this month to focus on instilling manners in the family:

- Designate at least one meal each week this month to work on table manners. Get the children involved with setting the table, if they're not already doing it.

- Using Galatians 5:22, 23: "The fruit of the Spirit is love, joy, peace, patience, kindness, goodness, faithfulness, gentleness and self-control" as a guide, choose two attributes to work on each week, with love as the guiding light all month.

- Take advantage of Mother's Day this month and Father's Day next month to give your children a special opportunity to dote on each parent, while also learning how to be spouses one day themselves.

For more ideas and books on instilling manners in your family, visit www.mannersoftheheart.org.

June
Have a Neighborhood Treasure Hunt

Why not organize a treasure hunt for the kids in your neighborhood? This will take a bit of work, but what a great summer project for the whole family.

Begin by choosing a Saturday for the big event. Draw a map of your neighborhood. Mark the cross streets and label houses by family names. If you're living in a high-rise, do the same by floors, instead of streets. Mark your place with an X. Add the date, time, and place for the treasure hunt. Make copies on parchment paper. Roll and tie with string, like an old treasure map. Have your kids deliver the announcements to your neighbors.

Next, make a list of treasures to be found for each age group represented: coins, leaves, feathers, lady bugs, rocks, a pebble smaller than a dime or larger than a dime, a clover leaf, grain of sand, Y-shaped twig, acorns or other nuts, and objects the kids can find in your area. Include the names and addresses of neighbors the kids can ask for an autograph or to answer questions, like "What's your favorite food?" or "Where were you born?"

Before all the kids head out on their hunting expedition, make a batch of cookies for them to package for neighbors who participate. On the big day, divide the children into teams by age. Teenagers can serve as team captains and take the youngest kids around the neighborhood. Give each team a list and a pen, along with a paper bag to collect their treasures. (You can pick up a clipboard for the question sheets at the Dollar Store.)

Use your imagination—this could become a new neighborhood tradition!

July
Celebrate the Red, White, and Blue

Celebrate the birth of our nation by celebrating the best of America this month. Make it a red, white, and blue month. Hang our country's flag on the front of your home or display it prominently inside your home. If this is your vacation month, replace a trip to the beach with a trip to our nation's capital. Visit www.washington.org to read about educational opportunities and fun for the whole family.

Not to worry, if a trip is not in the budget, you can enjoy good old-fashioned Americana in your own backyard:

- When was the last time you put everything aside on your weekend to-do list and went for a picnic? Gather the family, pack up, and head out. Don't forget the watermelon!

- Stage a Fourth of July parade on your street. Invite your friends and neighbors to join in.

    - Decorate tricycles, bicycles, or pull toys: Weave crepe paper through bicycle spokes, tie helium-filled balloons to handlebars with streamers, hang empty cans or pie plates from the back of the bikes.

- Turn a child's wagon into a float filled with stuffed animals.

- Add marching people with rhythm instruments and noisemakers.

- Play march music from a CD player.

- Serve vanilla ice cream with blueberries and strawberries on top for a patriotic summer dessert. Make cupcakes covered in icing with red, white, and blue sprinkles. Add an American flag.

- Brush up on your American history as a family. Discuss the following with your kids:

  - The thirteen original colonies

  - The presidents, in chronological order

  - The Declaration of Independence

  - The preamble to the Constitution

  - The Bill of Rights

  - The state capitals

  - Look for the "American Heritage Series," hosted by David Barton, on your local cable channel. The series presents America's forgotten history and heroes, emphasizing the moral, religious, and constitutional foundation on which America was built. The series (twenty-eight episodes) is available on DVD through www.wallbuilders .com.

- Pray together for the leaders of our nation.

Help your children appreciate the blessings we have in our country. Remind them that God has blessed us so that we may bless others.

August
Get to Know the Heroes of Our Faith

People are always telling your children what they should do with their lives. Kids are bombarded with enticing dollar signs, prestige, and power. Help them keep their feet on the ground and their mind pointed toward eternity by setting aside time this month to read about those who answered God's call for their lives.

Heroes of the Faith is a wonderful series from Barbour Publishing, comprised of books that tell the life stories of fifty people, including C. S. Lewis, Abraham Lincoln, Amy Carmichael, D. L. Moody, Florence Nightingale, Corrie ten Boom, Eric Liddell, and many more.

The Sower Series from Mott Media explores how Christianity influenced several of our country's great leaders: Daniel Webster, Florence Nightingale, George Washington, George Washington Carver, Robert E. Lee, and Stonewall Jackson, just to name a few. The story of Robert Boyle in *Trailblazer of Science* offers a stark contrast to the lives of those who place importance on riches. Boyle was born into a wealthy family of earls and dukes, but chose to live his life as a "Christian gentleman" scientist. His intent as a scientist was to direct attention to God for the ultimate explanations of nature. Boyle was highly respected in his field, and his writings are studied even today, three hundred years later.

Mary Slessor's biography, *Trial by Poison,* from the *Trailblazer Series* is a story of selflessness, commitment, and determined progress. Mary served Christ in Africa, following in the footsteps of her mentor, David Livingstone. She endured many hardships without complaint, and is an inspiring example of selflessness.

If you have teenagers, rent a few movies, such as:

- *Amazing Grace,* the story of William Wilberforce, the relentless politician who finally won freedom for slaves in 1807 after a twenty-year battle in the British Parliament.

- *Luther,* the story of the founder of the Protestant Reformation, Martin Luther.

- *Shadowlands,* the story of C. S. Lewis's journey of faith.

Your children will find these stories fascinating, and they will gain insight for overcoming controversy, adversity, and living selflessly for the cause of Christ.

September
Make a Homemade Bee Skep

Did you know that September is National Honey Month? Since Proverbs compares kind words to honey (16:24 NLT), September is a timely month for a family project that helps kids learn the importance of kind words.

Kids need to know that "An anxious heart weighs a man down, but a kind word cheers him up" (Proverbs 12:25). You can show your children this truth in your everyday interactions with others. Be kind with your words to everyone you meet: the homeless person on the street, your children's coach, your children's teacher, the wait person taking your order, the telemarketer on the phone, and on and on. Your children pay more attention to the way you talk to others than they do to you!

Together with your children make a homemade bee skep (beehive) to hold our "honey" words. Making a homemade bee skep isn't as complicated as it might sound. Cut a two-liter bottle in half, about ten inches from the base. Take the top portion, and help your children coil a lightweight rope around the base, beginning at the bottom. Glue the rope in place using a hot-glue gun. Continue wrapping until the bottle is covered, and then tuck the end of the rope in the top of the bottle.

Place your bee skep on a salad plate in a gathering spot in your home, such as the kitchen or den. Print the key verse, "Kind words are like honey—sweet to the soul and healthy for the body" (Proverbs 16:24 NLT) on a card so the family can memorize it this month.

Have your children make a list of thirty kind words or phrases. For example:

- Thank you
- Excuse me
- I'm sorry
- Way to go
- Forgive me
- You're welcome
- Good thinking!
- Please

Write the words on slips of paper and place them underneath the bee skep on the plate. Each morning have a family member choose a word of the day and encourage everyone in the family to use the word as many times as possible during the day. Repetition is the way to form new habits that will last beyond this month.

Below are three fun suggestions to add to the month's project:

- If you're feeling adventuresome, visit www.honeylocater .com to find a beekeeper in your area. The kids would love a field trip to see the real thing!

- Check out Max Lucado's *Hermie and Friends: Buzby the Misbehaving Bee* on DVD.

- Read *Gold & Honey* by Melody Carlson with your children.

October
Make Halloween Treats

We live on a cul-de-sac in a quiet neighborhood. For us, Halloween is a special night when the kids dress up while the neighbors visit. Last year one little girl not only told me, "Thank you very, very much," but gave me a hug to go with her words of gratitude.

I enjoy watching the trick-or-treaters count the number of pieces they take from the basket. I can tell which children have been given instructions to take only one or two pieces rather than a handful. The ones who take the least are the ones who always say "thank you." The kids who grab a handful are in such a hurry to make it to the next hit that they don't have time to show gratitude.

Why not spend October making Halloween treats for your kids to give while they are trick-or-treating? Who says kids can't offer a "thank you" treat in return for all that candy? Goodness, this idea might even make the evening news! Can't you see the headline: "Children *Giving* More Than They Get on Halloween Night!"

Here are a few ideas for making treats your children can share with others as they make their Halloween rounds:

- Invite your kids' friends over to make Halloween cards.

- Another day they could make sugar cookies using cookie cutters in fun shapes. Decorate them and place in clear bags. Tie the top with a twist tie or add tags with a Bible verse or friendly saying. Place in the freezer until Halloween night.

- How about making Halloween "crackers?" Have your kids cut empty toilet paper rolls or paper towel rolls in half, and then put a few pieces of candy in each roll, along with a

Bible verse. Cut three pieces of tissue paper in complementary colors, ten inches longer than the roll. Place the roll in the center of the tissue paper and roll it up! Tape the edge closed or use a sticker. Tie bright ribbons on the ends to hold the treats inside.

Don't leave your teenagers out of the Halloween festivities. Involve them in making the treats and giving out to younger children.

November
Count Your Blessings

In 1789 George Washington began his Thanksgiving proclamation for our country with these words:

> Whereas it is the duty of all nations to acknowledge the providence of Almighty God, to obey His will, to be grateful for His benefits, and humbly implore His protection, aid and favors. . . . Now, therefore, I do recommend and assign Thursday, the 26th day of November next, to be devoted by the people of these states to the service of that great and glorious Being, who is the Beneficent Author of all the good that was, that is, or that will be; that we may then all unite in rendering unto Him our sincere and humble thanks for His kind care and protection of the people of this country, and for all the great and various favors which He has been pleased to confer upon us.[5]

Our children will probably never hear this proclamation in school. It is our duty to teach them. Let's use the month of November to follow our first president's mandate to be grateful for the many blessings the "glorious Being" has bestowed upon us.

Here are a few suggestions:

- Pick up at least three dozen inexpensive solid-colored Christmas balls and paint pens. Starting on November 1, ask family members to write down something or someone they're thankful for on the balls each day. Collect them in a large bowl or basket as the month progresses. On Thanksgiving Day have your children count the many blessings of the family as they name them one by one. (You can have your kids tie ribbon on the balls and hang them on your Christmas tree the next month.)

- Thanksgiving afternoon have a few inexpensive baskets, apple Christmas ornaments, and straw stuffing ready for your children to make a basket of apple ornaments to give to friends. Help your children write the names of the family members on the apples, using white paint. Fill a basket with straw stuffing and apples. Include a card printed with the sentiment: "You're the apple of His eye" (based on Deuteronomy 32:10).

- Send an e-card each day from the family to someone special "just because"—maybe relatives, long-lost friends, grandparents, neighbors, your government officials (the mayor, school board members, principals, teachers, ministers, senators and representatives, the president, vice-president, and so on). It doesn't cost a thing, but a little bit of time. The benefit for your children—priceless.

December
Focus on the True Gift of Christmas

Don't allow the holidays to pull you apart. Gather your children near. I bet you'll find something on the "twenty-four days of Christmas" list that will help you focus on the true gift of Christmas—love. You can start a new tradition.

- Day 1—Start reading A *Christmas Carol* aloud as a family.

- Day 2—Help the children go through their toys to give away to needy children.

- Day 3—Participate in Heifer International by providing a work animal for a family in poverty at www.heifer.org or Samaritan's purse to help children at www.samaritanspurse .org

- Day 4—Adopt a family for Christmas.

- Day 5—Make a batch of homemade jelly to share with sanitation workers and the mailman.

- Day 6—Invite kids over to make candy houses.

- Day 7—Make homemade Christmas cards and send them out.

- Day 8—Let your kids add a canned good to the food pantry with each visit to the grocery.

- Day 9—Adopt an elderly neighbor.

- Day 10—Have a special prayer time for the homeless.

- Day 11—Make a family newspaper, *The Christmas Clarion*. Let the kids interview members of the family to record Christmas memories from days gone by.

- Day 12—Make homemade gifts for each member of the family.

- Day 13—Host a birthday party for Jesus. Invite children to come with a gift that will be given to children in need.

- Day 14—Let the children write and perform a Christmas play for the neighborhood.

- Day 15—Sing Christmas carols around the dinner table.

- Day 16—Make homemade bread from scratch, no machines!

- Day 17—Watch *It's a Wonderful Life* with fresh popped corn.

- Day 18—Take the family and friends to visit a live nativity scene.

- Day 19—Make old-fashioned popcorn garlands for the tree and kitchen windows.

- Day 20—Let the children go door to door, taking candy canes to neighbors with a special sentiment attached. (Read *The Candymaker's Gift* for ideas.)

- Day 21—Have a candlelight supper around the Christmas tree.

- Day 22—Make a list of family promises to each other for the new year.

- Day 23—Read the Christmas story from Luke 2.

- Day 24—Attend a Christmas Eve service at your local church.

- Christmas morning—Make a birthday cake for Jesus! Don't forget to sing "Happy Birthday"!

During the Christmas season add a "Happy Birthday" to your greeting. Jesus asks us to celebrate His coming, accept His gift of salvation, and share His message with others. This is a wonderful opportunity to share Jesus with others and teach your children a lesson in showing Jesus's love to others.

Merry Christmas and Happy Birthday to you and yours!

———————

After a year of intentionally working at becoming a family that plays together and prays together, you'll find the satisfaction that can be found in family togetherness. Our homes are meant to be a place of refuge from the world, not a battleground. Remember what Dorothy said at the end of *The Wizard of Oz*? She was right: "There's no place like home." If you don't feel that way, do something about it.

CHAPTER 9

Educate the Heart in Forgiveness

I WILL NEVER FORGET the lesson portrayed in the movie *The Emperor's Club*, which is based on Ethan Canin's short story "The Palace Thief." Sedgewick Bell, the cocky son of a powerful West Virginia senator, was sent to an elite all-boys boarding school for an education befitting his heritage and intelligence. But his poor attitude and mischievous behavior labeled him a troublemaker the first day he arrived on campus. Professor Hundert, an amiable English teacher filled with a deep desire to mold his students into men of character, took a special interest in Sedgewick. The professor visited Senator Bell in his Washington office to discuss his son's troubles.

As Professor Hundert attempted to explain his concerns, it became quite obvious to him that the senator cared only about his son's academic score. He didn't care how his son got to the top of the class, only that he did. The senator admonished Hundert not to concern himself with Sedgewick's character, saying, "You're to teach my son, not to mold him. I will mold my own son."

And mold him he did.

Nonetheless, Professor Hundert and Sedgewick began to develop a close relationship. Sedgewick appeared to be inspired. He buckled down to his studies, and his grades improved—but not enough to land him a spot in the prestigious Julius Caesar academic competition. So Hundert bent the rules by raising Sedgewick's grade on the final essay so that he could secure a spot in the competition. Later the professor regretted this compromise of his integrity.

During the competition Sedgewick answered one question after another with pointed accuracy and made it to the final round. But when Hundert realized that Sedgewick had cheated his way through the contest, the professor chose a final question he was certain Sedgewick would be unable to answer on his own and that his opponent would know. Sure enough, Sedgewick was stumped and the other student won. When Sedgewick lost the competition, his father looked on in disgust—not because his son had cheated, but because he had lost.

Many of Professor Hundert's student went on to great success in their careers and personal lives, attributing their successes to their teacher's tutelage, but the professor never recovered from his disappointment in Sedgewick. Twenty-five years after that telling competition, Sedgewick, who had gone on to great wealth in the business world, asked for another chance at the competition, and he invited Professor Hundert to officiate. Former classmates and their families gathered at a posh resort for a reunion and a rematch. Before the match, Sedgewick tells Hundert how his influence had changed his life and that he wanted to regain Hundert's respect, which was why he'd asked for a rematch. Hundert allowed himself to believe that Sedgewick had changed.

But he hadn't. Sedgewick not only cheated his way through the competition again, but he also used the weekend to announce to his former classmates, many of whom were now wealthy, that he was running for his father's senate seat and to raise money. Ironically, no one except Professor Hundert knew Sedgewick's true character. The senator had educated his son's heart well. He'd taught him to say the right thing at the right time in order to achieve his goals, to use people for his selfish pursuits, and to apologize for nothing.

Shortly after Sedgewick's announcement, Hundert confronted Sedgewick in the men's room. With arrogance and indignation in his voice, Sedgewick told Professor Hundert that it really didn't matter that he cheated his way through life because "life is full of cheaters." As the words fell from his mouth, a stall door opened to reveal his young son, who had been listening to every word. The boy looked into his father's eyes with heartbreaking disappointment. Sedgewick tried to speak, but nothing came out. His son lowered his head in shame as he walked past his fallen hero.

Sedgewick Bell's father wanted power, prestige, and position for his son. He didn't care what his son had to do to get to the top, as long as he got there. He was more concerned that his son *look* good than *be* good. Sadly, his son learned those heart lessons all too well. His heart was full of selfishness, greed, and deceit.

PARENTS DETERMINE THE CONTENT OF THEIR CHILD'S HEART

Proverbs tells us: "As water reflects a face, so a man's heart reflects the man" (27:19). As Christians it's our sacred duty and holy honor to develop our children's hearts to be reflections of Christ. To do so, we must invest time and love in our kids. There is no substitute for either.

Mamie Gene Cole explained it best in the last stanza of "I Am the Child," a poem she penned as a young child speaking to her parents:

> You hold in your hand the key to my heart and my destiny,
> You can determine largely whether I shall succeed or fail.
> Give me, I beg you, all those things that make for true
>   happiness.

Train me, I beg you, so that I may become a blessing to the world.[1]

You know you have heartwork to do if . . .

- Your five-year-old has a temper tantrum when you ask her to share her toys. Her heart needs a filling of *generosity.*

- Your sixteen-year-old is never satisfied and suffers from chronic boredom. His heart needs a load of *gratitude.*

- Your ten-year-old has trouble keeping friends. Her heart is void of *forgiveness.*

Our typical response when we see these struggles in our children is to ask them questions like these:

- "What were you thinking?"

- "Why can't you study harder?"

- "What's wrong with you?"

- "Why can't you learn to get along?"

The content of their hearts will determine your children's decisions and actions. Scripture tells us the heart drives the mind. David understood that God knows our hearts better than we do, and he gave his son this expert advice:

And you, Solomon my son, get to know well your father's God; serve him with a whole heart and eager mind, for God examines every heart and sees through every motive. If you seek him, he'll make sure you find him, but if you abandon him, he'll leave you for good. Look sharp now! God has chosen *you* to build his holy house. Be brave, determined! And do it! (1 Chronicles 28:9–10 MSG)

God has a plan for each of your children, a unique task for each one. It is your duty to prepare their hearts to accept His call. Your job isn't to make your children happy, but to lead them toward holiness. Your job isn't to make your children good, but to lead them toward godliness. Your job is to bump your children off self-center and to encourage them to be all that God created them to be.

HEARTWORK PRAYER FOR YOUR CHILDREN

I pray that out of his glorious riches
he may strengthen [your child's name]
with power through his Spirit in his inner being,
so that Christ may dwell in [your child's name]
heart through faith.
And I pray that [your child's name],
being rooted and established in love,
may have power together with all the saints,
to grasp how wide and long and high
and deep is the love of Christ,
and to know this love that surpasses knowledge—
that he may be filled to the measure
of all the fullness of God.
EPHESIANS 3:16–19

Mark it down: our children's hearts determine their attitudes, behavior, actions, and reactions. What's in your children's hearts?

I believe parents can foster three fundamental qualities that can set children's hearts in the right direction: forgiveness, generosity, and gratitude.

- *Forgiveness* will transform a ten-year-old who holds grudges against her friends into a young person who readily forgives and forgets.

- *Generosity* will transform a five-year-old who has trouble sharing his toys into a child who finds more joy in giving than receiving.

- *Gratitude* will transform a sixteen-year-old who is always asking for more into a young person who appreciates what she does have.

It's critical that you cultivate these qualities in the hearts of your children, and for that reason we're going to spend the rest of this chapter looking at *forgiveness*. Then we'll spend the next chapter talking about *generosity* and *gratitude*.

TEACHING FORGIVENESS

If you've read *Raising Respectful Children in a Disrespectful World*, you know my husband left home the week our twin sons entered sixth grade. After a year of living away from us, he came home one night to tell us of his decision to end the marriage. We told him how much we loved him and pleaded with him to stay home, but he drove away convinced it was the only thing he could do. I lay awake all night, holding my precious twelve-year-old sons as they slept, asking the Lord for His wisdom and strength to raise boys with forgiving hearts, protected from bitterness.

Before their dad left home I wakened the boys every morning by singing a little melody God had written on my heart when they started school. Rather than an alarm clock, my boys had what they called a "momalarm." During the year their dad lived away from home, I didn't have the energy or motivation to be their "momalarm." At this point it had been months since they had heard it.

During the night as I begged the Lord for strength to carry on, He filled the wound of my heart with His love and sealed it with His mercy. He answered my cry for help. When the first light of day pierced through the darkness, His light awakened my soul to a new dawn in my spirit. The impossible was possible . . . I could sing again. Not because the pain was gone, but because the Healer had come.

The words of that sweet melody sang from the depths of my being in a new way, a fresh way, with deeper meaning than ever before:

> It's a bright and beautiful day.
> God made it special that way.
> We're gonna' sing and shout His name.
> Hosanna, praise His name.
> And if your day gets tough,
> Just remember to look above;
> And Jesus will shine His love on you.
> I said, Jesus will shine His love on you.
> I said, Jesus will shine His love on you.
> Yes, He will.

My boys both opened their eyes and smiled with sheepish grins that had long been missing. As I leaned over to kiss their cheeks, one of them said, "Mom, Mom, God put our song back in your heart. Everything's gonna be okay. He's here with us."

At the breakfast table we made a promise to pray for each other every day, and that together we would pray for their dad every morning. In the months that followed, I discovered you cannot despise someone you are praying for. When bitterness would attempt to enter my heart, I would pray for deeper love. On nights when my strength was gone, the boys would offer to tuck *me* in bed, an opportunity to show their increasing maturity and tender-heartedness through a sweet gesture of compassion in the midst of their pain.

God amazed me in the way He protected the boys from bitterness. His protection came through a profound understanding of His command to "love the sinner and hate the sin." When anger overwhelmed them, they could rightly hate the sin, while praying for more love for the one who had disappointed them. God protected their souls with the shield of forgiveness.

Of all the blessings God granted us during this difficult season, He enabled us to love as He loves and to forgive as He forgives. This preserved our hearts. Forgiveness kept pain from turning to bitterness.

HOW TO FORGIVE

In *Secure in the Everlasting Arms,* Elisabeth Elliot outlines five steps for how to forgive others when they have offended you in some way:

1. *Acknowledge the sin, apart from the sinner.* Call sin what it is—sin. Love the person, but don't excuse the sin.

2. *Take it to God in prayer.* Don't tell others about the offense. Keep it between you and God. You cannot hold a grudge if you begin praying for the person who has hurt you.

3. *Ask God for mercy and love.* Pray not only for mercy for the offender, but for more love in your heart. Ask God in His great mercy and love to enable you to forgive fully and completely.

4. *If led to confront the offender, do so in grace, truth, and love.* Only go to the offender if God leads you to do so. The only reason to extend forgiveness to that person is for his or her sake. Too often we run to the other person to make ourselves feel better, pushing the person farther away from God. Forgive the person in your heart, then lay it down at the cross. More times than not, just take care of the matter between you and the Lord. Then love the offender wisely, with God's love.

5. *Tell the offender you've forgiven him or her.* True forgiveness is received as love from the offender. When forgiveness is given with the right heart attitude, grace abounds.

That's why it is so important that our kids know how to offer forgiveness as well as request forgiveness.

Unless our own hearts are filled with forgiveness, we will not be able to cultivate forgiveness in the hearts of our children.

MODELING FORGIVENESS

I'll say it again; children learn best by example. That means you need to offer an apology or ask for forgiveness when you do things like the following:

- Hang up the phone, knowing you offended the person on the other end of the line.

- Avoid someone because you have been dishonest with that person.

- Are harsh with one of your children rather than firm.

It's never too late to show remorse to someone you've wronged, wounded, offended, or upset. It's important for your children to see you humble yourself and admit when you've been wrong, whether it's to their grandparent, the mailman, a clerk in a store, or to one of them.

The best way you can plant and water the seed of forgiveness in your children's hearts is by:

1. *Forgiving them when they do wrong.* Forgive your children quickly when they do wrong against you, but don't remove the consequences for their misbehavior.

   Children need to be reprimanded when they do wrong, and they need to suffer the consequences. Discomfort motivates us to change. If your kids don't suffer any negative consequences for their misbehavior, they won't be inspired to change.

2. *Forgiving others when they offend you.* This is another way your kids can see forgiveness in action, one that is up close and personal. Let your kids see you quickly forgive small offenses.

   Rather than complaining about your neighbor who can't seem to remember not to put away his garbage can every week after garbage pickup, move the can yourself and put it in the place he keeps it, as a way of forgiving the offense. (Does it really matter that much? I bet it won't be long before your neighbor is taking care of it.)

   Rather than rolling your eyes at the woman who cuts in front of you in the line at Wal-Mart or huffing and puffing when someone takes the parking space you were waiting for, graciously let her have it. Wouldn't it be great for your kids to hear you say, "She must be in a really big hurry," instead of, "Who does she think she is?"

Even in the "big" offenses, we can choose forgiveness. A businessman I had turned to for advice decided rather than advise me, he would write a letter outlining my faults and why I would not succeed in my venture. When he sent the letter to a few select recipients, I was not only angry but embarrassed. I prayed, asking for an open heart. By the time the boys came in from school, I had called the gentleman and thanked him for laying out my weaknesses, because it enabled me to identify the areas where I would need to find help to succeed.

We have become so consumed with ourselves in today's self-absorbed world, we sometimes think we have to "punish" others by withholding our forgiveness—as if that will make a difference in their behavior. Our children desperately need to see us model forgiveness in our relationships.

Your children will do what they see you doing in this area. If you are unforgiving, they, too, will withhold forgiveness. If you are forgiving, they will find it much easier to forgive.

The moment you recognize you're carrying a grudge or feel bitterness looming in your heart, correct it. If you can't forgive, ask God to help you forgive. If you're willing to let go of your resentment, He is more than pleased to help you forgive. All He ever needs from us is a willing spirit.

3. *Asking your kids for forgiveness when you wrong them.* A friend of mine has mastered this lesson. One evening Nancy finally agreed to help her teenage daughter, Becky, finish a tough school project. Mentally patting herself on

the back, Nancy turned to leave Becky's room, and noticed what a mess it was. Without thinking she scolded, "This room is a disaster—you better get . . ." She glanced back at her daughter, but the words stuck in her throat. The sparkle in Becky's eyes from the satisfaction of a finished school project dimmed. Nancy shot an "arrow" prayer to ask for God's help in the situation.

"Becky, I messed up—and I'm so sorry. Please forgive me for those discouraging words. I felt so proud about being a good mom and helping you with your project that I let it go to my head. This wasn't the time to add anything more to your plate. Will you please forgive me?" she said to her daughter.

Becky had no problem forgiving her mom. She crossed the room and gave her a hug, saying, "Thank you for admitting when you're wrong. You are a good example for me."

Along with modeling forgiveness, it's important you teach your children how to ask for forgiveness.

Therefore, as God's chosen people, holy and dearly loved,
clothe yourselves with compassion, kindness,
humility, gentleness and patience.
Bear with each other and forgive whatever grievances
you may have against one another.
Forgive as the Lord forgave you.
COLOSSIANS 3:12, 13

TEACHING CHILDREN TO ASK FOR FORGIVENESS

In *Kids With Character,* author and educator Marti Garlett tells how one mom taught her daughter to ask for forgiveness. Six-year-old Marcy was enthralled by a new display of miniature playing cards at her favorite dime store. When her mom told her they had to leave, a box of cards left with them—in Marcy's front pocket.

When they got home, Marcy went into the bathroom so she could admire her cards in secret. When her older sister wanted in, Marcy eventually opened the door and couldn't resist showing off her new cards, saying that their mother had bought them for her. Of course, her sister knew better, and she told their mom about the box of cards.

"Well, there's only one thing to do," Marcy's mother said decisively, "Take them back to Mr. Sam right now, this very minute."

Marcy dreaded facing Mr. Sam, the store owner. When they arrived at the store, she followed her mom straight to Mr. Sam. Before Marcy could open her mouth, her mother said, "Mr. Sam, Marcy has something to tell you."

"I took these cards," she said, as she sat them on the counter in front of Mr. Sam.

"You didn't pay for them, did you, Marcy?" her mother prodded.

"No," said Marcy.

"And we don't take things we don't pay for, do we?"

"No," said Marcy.

"Tell Mr. Sam how sorry you are for taking something without paying for it."

Marcy took a deep breath to keep her tears away. "I'm sorry," she said.

Mr. Sam took the cards in the palm of his hand and with a curt nod said, "Thank you."

Back on the street, Marcy couldn't hold her tears any longer. Her mother took her in her arms and held her close. She smoothed her daughter's hair and said, "I love you, Marcy, I love you very, very much." [2]

Marcy's mother handled this tough moment as a loving parent should. Marcy had wronged someone and needed to make it right.

Even young children can learn that it isn't enough just to say "I'm sorry" when we do something wrong. We must be repentant of our wrongdoing and reach out to the person we've wronged to make amends. Scripture tells us, "Therefore, if you are offering your gift at the altar and there remember that your brother has something against you, leave your gift there in front of the altar. First go and be reconciled to your brother; then come and offer your gift" (Matthew 5:23–24).

When we teach our children to show remorse, repent, and apologize, then the process of forgiveness is complete:

- *Remorse*—I feel the pain I've caused. Your child regrets the damage that he or she has caused, not just sorrow for getting caught.

- *Repentance*—I turn away from the wrong action. Your child promises not to "do it" again, and then asks for God's help to live up to that promise.

- *Apology*—I ask to be forgiven. Your child asks the person he or she offended for forgiveness.

Children as young as two years old can understand the concept of feeling remorse for doing something wrong and should apologize. Once your kids are in school, insist that they be specific when apologizing for an offense and that they seek reconciliation with the person they hurt. For example, instead of just saying, "I'm sorry," teach them to say, "I'm sorry I took your truck and pushed you down, and I won't do it again." If your child is cruel to another child, make sure your child apologizes, gives a hug, and then offers to share one of his or her toys. The heart becomes engaged when we demonstrate the meaning of our words through our actions.

By the time your children hit the tween years, they're ready to go beyond seeking reconciliation to making restitution. For instance, if your son breaks a window or damages property, insist that he "make it right" by repairing the damage out of his own pocket. This is a time when Mom and Dad's greatest duty is *not* to help their child. Stand with your child and encourage but *don't* enable. If your child doesn't have the money, insist he or she earn the money by doing extra work around the house. If you enable your child by covering the cost yourself or taking care of the problem, you'll set a pattern that will be detrimental to your child's development. This is a time when heart lessons must be learned the hard way.

Stories about forgiveness can reinforce the lessons you are instilling in your kids' hearts about forgiveness. Use your Bible and your storytelling ability to read the Old Testament story of Joseph, beginning in Genesis 30. (When you tell stories without using picture books, it encourages children to use their imaginations.) Your children can learn many lessons from Joseph: He was a bit overconfident and spoiled as a boy, making him the envy of his ten older brothers. But he learned his heart lessons, particularly the lesson of forgiveness, and he grew to become a wise young man admired by all who knew him.

> If you have done your fellow a little wrong,
> let it be in your eyes great.
> If you have done him much good,
> let it be in your eyes little.
> If he has done you a little good,
> let it be in your eyes great.
> And if he has done you a great wrong,
> let it be in your eyes little.
> THE JEWISH TALMUD

Here are a few good books you can read with children to help instill forgiveness in their hearts:

- *LarryBoy and the Mudslingers,* by Doug Peterson, is the companion book to the Veggie Tales' *LarryBoy and the Bad Apple* video. It's a wonderful day at the Cannonball Water

Park—until the Bad Apple and her slimy sidekick, Curly, trick Laura Carrot and Junior Asparagus into starting a mud fight. One thing leads to another, and soon everyone is covered in mud! Kids will enjoy being a part of the fun as LarryBoy discovers the power of forgiveness.

- *Bad Day for Christopher Bear,* by Stephanie Jeffs, a British children's author, is a charming book about a boy named Joe who's having a rotten day. Joe is feeling cross, but it's also a bad day for his best friend, Christopher Bear. By the end of the day Joe knows that his sour attitude hurt those around him, and most of all, God. Joe learns to apologize to his friends and ask God's forgiveness.

- *Pearl and Wagner: Two Good Friends,* by Kate McMullan, is a delightful story that stresses the importance of friendship. Pearl, a hardworking rabbit, and Wagner, a daydreaming mouse, build a robot together for the school science fair. Sometimes a robot doesn't turn out quite the way it's supposed to, and sometimes a pair of new green boots can cause a fight. Through it all, Pearl and Wagner show that they know how to forgive and forget and stay good friends, no matter what.

When your children enter middle school and high school, they are ready for deeper lessons in forgiveness.

HELPING TEENS UNDERSTAND THE NECESSITY OF FORGIVENESS

Angela came in from school singing the blues. She wasn't practicing for an audition, but bemoaning her "former" best friend, LeeAnn. It seems LeeAnn heard an ugly rumor about Angela, and rather than coming to her for confirmation, she joined with others in spreading the nasty tale. Angela was so angry, she never wanted to speak to Lee-Ann again.

Two weeks passed. The rumor proved to be untrue and was long forgotten, but Angela was still avoiding LeeAnn, who had never apologized for her thoughtlessness. Angela had decided it would be easier to find a new best friend than to forgive LeeAnn. Another two weeks passed. Angela continued searching for someone to agree with her anger. Friends stopped calling to go out because they were tired of hearing about "what LeeAnn did."

Angela was caught in the trap of unforgiveness. She needed to hear Paul's words to the Romans who were struggling with unforgiveness:

Do not repay anyone evil for evil. Be careful to do what is right in the eyes of everybody. If it is possible, as far as it depends on you, live at peace with everyone. Do not take revenge, my friends, but leave room for God's wrath, for it is written: "It is mine to avenge; I will repay," says the Lord. On the contrary: If your enemy is hungry, feed him; if he is thirsty, give him something to drink. In doing this, you will heap burning coals on his head. Do not be overcome by evil, but overcome evil with good. (Romans 12:14–21)

Your teens need to know that by holding unforgiveness in their hearts, they're keeping the wound of the offense open. They're not allowing God to heal the wound. It is our forgiveness that brings healing, not the other person's apology. That's why God calls us to love and forgive others, regardless of their actions.

This is tough stuff for us and tough stuff for our teens. But tough stuff is good stuff, because learning to forgive as God's Word teaches is a lesson that transforms lives from ordinary to extraordinary.

Let me encourage you to share with your teens the consequences of unforgiveness. Here's the inevitable progression:

1. I am unwilling to forgive.

2. I become bitter, causing me more pain than the original offense.

3. I'm now held in bondage to the one I want to be free from.

4. Others move away from me because the bitterness permeates all areas of my life.

5. The Lord can't work in the other person's life because I'm standing in the way.

6. The Lord can't bless me, until I'm willing to allow Him to help me forgive.

If we fail to forgive, we're the ones who will suffer, just as Angela discovered.

Now, share with your teen three good reasons why we must forgive others:

1. God's Word is clear. He tells us to forgive.

2. When we forgive, our wounded heart will heal. Forgiveness and redemption go hand in hand.

3. When we forgive the one who has wronged us, we are showing that person the love of Christ.

What if Angela was your daughter? Would you agree with her or would you encourage her to take her hurt and pain to the foot of the cross, and ask God to help her forgive LeeAnn, whether her friend ever asks for forgiveness or not?

Keep in mind that teens are astute when it comes to finding excuses for not forgiving others. Here are some common excuses, as well as help for how to respond.

- *"I don't feel like forgiving."* Feelings follow action. We don't forgive because we have a warm fuzzy feeling in our heart toward the other person; we forgive because we love God. Feelings catch up to the action because forgiveness is a godly quality, not a human emotion. Alexander Pope was right when he said, "To err is human, to forgive divine."

- *"But what they did was wrong."* Forgiveness doesn't excuse the other person's sin. The other person must answer to God. We should pray for mercy, not seek revenge.

- *"I can't forget about it."* We may not be able to forget about the hurt, but we can live past it. Scripture tells us to live in peace with others. This means we are to forgive them, even if we remember the hurt.

DEALING WITH CHILD ABUSE

If your child has been sexually or physically abused by someone, you must protect your child by reporting the offender to the police and taking your child out of harm's way. You must also protect your child's heart by getting him or her the professional help needed for healing.

Statistics show there are unfortunate long-term effects for children whose hearts have not been healed from abuse:

- Abused children are 25 percent more likely to experience teen pregnancy.

- Children who experience child abuse and neglect are 59 percent more likely to be arrested as a juvenile, 28 percent more likely to be arrested as an adult, and 30 percent more likely to commit violent crime.

- Of all men in prison in the United States, 14.4 percent were abused as children, and 36.7 percent of all women in prison were abused as children.

- Children who have been sexually abused are 2.5 times more likely develop alcohol abuse.

- Children who have been sexually abused are 3.8 times more likely develop drug addictions.

- Nearly two-thirds of the people in treatment for drug abuse reported being abused as children.[3]

The Childhelp National Child Abuse Hotline is available twenty-four hours a day, seven days a week at (800) 4A-CHILD. For further information, contact: Childhelp USA, 15757 North 78th Street, Scottsdale, Arizona 85260. For additional help, The Billy Graham Evangelistic Association suggests the books *Pain and Pretending*, by Rich Buhler, and *Helping Victims of Sexual Abuse*, by Jeannette Vought and Lynn Heitritter, available at most Christian bookstores.

You can also teach your teens about forgiveness through certain books and films. For example, *Les Misérables,* which is both a book and a movie as well as a Broadway play, is a beautiful story of forgiveness and generosity. Jean Valjean is released from a French prison after serving nineteen years for stealing a loaf of bread and for subsequent attempts to escape from prison. The kindly bishop of Digne, Myriel, treats Valjean with kindness, but Valjean repays the bishop by stealing his silverware. When the police arrest Valjean, Myriel covers for him, claiming that the silverware was a gift and then added a pair of valuable silver candlesticks to what he'd stolen. The authorities release Valjean, and Myriel makes him promise to become an honest man.

Eager to fulfill his promise, Valjean masks his identity and enters the town of Montreuil-sur-mer. Under the assumed name of Madeleine, Valjean invents an ingenious manufacturing process that brings the town prosperity. He eventually becomes the town's mayor.

Your teenage daughter would enjoy reading *Redeeming Love*, by Francine Rivers, which is a beautiful retelling of the story of Hosea, one of the greatest stories of forgiveness, in Scripture. The story is set in the Gold Rush days of the 1850s.

Forgiveness is hard, but not impossible with God's help. Your children can become graceful forgivers who reach out to others with love. I know, because my precious sons taught their mother more than I could ever have taught them about forgiveness.

A LESSON IN FORGIVENESS

When our twin sons were four years old, our family moved to Manhattan. One of my most vivid memories of our New York days happened just after our first Thanksgiving in the city. We left the apartment early one morning to make the long trek to 34th Street to see Macy's animated Christmas village. It was worth the effort; the boys were mesmerized. Mom was, too.

We took our time coming home, wandering up Fifth Avenue, stopping to admire the window displays. We were only a couple of blocks from our apartment building when the boys were ready for a snack. We stopped at a corner store we often frequented.

Inside the shop customers were standing in a long line, waiting to buy lottery tickets. Undaunted, the boys made their food selections, and we stepped to the back of the line.

When it was our turn to pay, I said hello to the gentleman behind the counter and prompted the boys to do the same. I handed him a twenty-dollar bill and waited for change. When he gave me change as if I had given him a five-dollar bill, I hesitated, looked in my empty wallet, and told him he had been mistaken, that I had given him a twenty.

He began yelling at me. Told me to get out of his store. Threatened that if I didn't leave, he would call the police, because I was trying to "run a scam." I was mortified, humiliated. Confused, the boys asked what I had done to make the man so angry.

As we hurried past the line of customers, an older lady tugged my arm and said, "You should be ashamed of yourself, in front of your children."

Tears clouded my vision as the boys and I ran back to our building. The elevator to the fifteenth floor seemed to take twice as long as usual. When we finally entered our apartment, I dropped my purse and collapsed in the comfort of the nearest chair. The boys crawled into my lap, wrapping their arms around me with those wonderful "little boy" hugs.

"He just got mixed up," Chad said.

"He was too busy to think right," Boyce added.

"It's all right, Mom. We know the truth. Let's pray he won't get mixed up again," said Chad.

That wasn't my prayer of choice, but Boyce wiped away my tears, and the three of us bowed our heads to ask for strength to forgive.

Months later, we were headed home when Chad stopped dead in

his tracks. "Mom," he exclaimed. "Did you ever tell that man you forgave him for yelling at you?" I looked up to see we were standing in front of the corner store.

"Well, I haven't been back in the store," I said, trying to escape Chad's question.

Boyce looked at me with that face only your child can give you. "Well, Mom . . . it seems to me that he'll never know you forgave him unless you go in and tell him. Isn't that what you tell us?"

He was right.

"Okay, let's go in. We'll even buy a snack," I said. (Yes, I checked my wallet for one-dollar bills before we walked in!)

The boys beamed with pride as we walked up to the owner, who was behind the counter. His bewildered look revealed he remembered us. As we completed our transaction, I hesitated, cleared my throat, and said, "I want you to know that I forgave you for accusing me unjustly a few months ago." He nodded affirmatively, his face void of expression. I turned to the boys as we were leaving and reminded them to "tell the nice man to have a good day."

When we stepped on the sidewalk Boyce patted my back and said, "Good job, Mom. Now, doesn't that feel good?"

Isn't it amazing how our kids can teach us the lessons we've been trying to teach them?

CHAPTER 10

Educate the Heart in Generosity and Gratitude

It was the week before Christmas, and the boys and I were finishing our deliveries of Christmas "happies." We headed upstairs in our apartment building to make a delivery to the last family on our list. The boys knocked, the door opened, and on cue we blurted out "Merrrrrrry Christmas." I was holding a homemade gift basket—nothing fancy or expensive—coffee mugs with hot chocolate mix, a tiny gift for each of the three children.

"What is it with you?" the stunned recipient questioned. "You're always baking cookies or bringing meals to people. I, for one, don't want to be indebted to you. No, thank you."

The boys stared at me in disbelief as I stared at a woman who dared to be so ungrateful in front of my children. After regaining my Christmas spirit I said, "I'm sorry you feel that way. We just wanted to spread a little Christmas cheer. Let's go, boys." The door closed.

My bottom lip began to quiver as we walked to the elevator. Just as the door opened, one of the boys took the basket from my hands and said, "Mom, we should leave it anyway. She really needs it."

The boys ran like sneaky little Christmas mice down the hallway to place the basket at our neighbor's door. They couldn't conceal their grins when they jumped on the elevator to go home.

This was generosity in action. My sons were generous grace givers when they offered undeserved favor to one who had been so ungrateful and unkind.

One of the blessings of educating your children's hearts is that rather than being wounded when others treat them poorly, they will walk away with hearts filled to overflowing with God's love. Something divine takes place on earth when grace is freely given from a forgiving and generous heart.

In the previous chapter we talked about instilling forgiveness in your children's hearts, and in this one we'll look at how you can educate their hearts in generosity as well as gratitude.

CULTIVATING GENEROSITY

I often ask parents what kind of children they want to raise. The usual answers are happy, kind, generous, strong, and smart. Recently a gentleman left me speechless when he replied, "Magnanimous. I want to raise magnanimous children." Now, that happens to be one of my all-time favorite words, but I rarely hear it used today. I've never heard it used in reference to children.

When I asked him to elaborate, he explained, "I'm so sick and tired of bratty kids that think the only pleasure in life comes from using a credit card to buy whatever they want. I want my kids to give more than they get."

I don't remember the last time I heard someone say to their boss, "You're a magnanimous leader." Or to their spouse, "Honey, you're the most magnanimous hubby I know." The word sounds as big as its meaning—"showing or suggesting nobility of feeling and generosity of mind, showing or suggesting a lofty and courageous spirit."

Imagine a generation of children who are generous in mind and spirit. Wouldn't it be thrilling to label the next generation The Magnanimous Generation! Much better than the "Me" Generation currently in vogue.

As a parent, you can do something to help make this happen in the hearts of your own children. Generosity is the outward expression of the condition of the heart. Children who give freely have hearts filled with the right stuff. Generosity leaves no room for greediness or selfishness. Kids find it hard to focus on themselves when they're looking for ways to give to others.

Selfish children can't bless the world, but unselfish children can shower the world with blessings. Take a look at the qualities found in a selfish child versus the qualities found in an unselfish child:

Selfish Child	**Unselfish Child**
• Demanding	• Empathetic
• Arrogant	• Grace-filled
• Holds grudges	• Forgiving
• Unappreciative	• Grateful
• Stingy	• Generous
• Lazy	• Helpful

How, then, do we cultivate generous, unselfish children?

TEACH THEM TO LIVE WITH OPEN HANDS AND OPEN HEARTS

One perfect spring morning girls dressed in puffy-sleeved dresses and boys in gingham-checked rompers came through the garden gate for the annual Easter egg hunt. In their hands were wicker baskets strewn with ribbons blowing in the gentle breeze. When the bell rang the children were off, squealing with delight with each new "find." As they pranced through the yard hunting for hidden eggs, they looked more like princes and princesses in a fairy tale than ordinary children.

They had just finished egg collecting when a little girl appeared at the gate with her mother. The mother apologized for being forty-five minutes late. Her daughter just stood there with her empty basket, looking at the other children. Her bottom lip began to quiver when she realized all their baskets were filled with eggs. No one knew what to say.

Before the girl's tears could fall, one of the moms encouraged her daughter to move forward and put eggs from her basket into the little girl's. She did, and soon all the children were transferring eggs from their baskets to that of the latecomer. One of the young boys brought a chocolate bunny from the refreshment table while another offered the girl a cup of lemonade.

Mothers were brimming with pride at the actions of their children. The wise mom who had prompted her daughter said, "I want my daughter to be a giver. Did you see her face when she gave away her eggs? She felt good on the inside."

You've heard the expression "give till it hurts." We want our children to "give till it feels good."

Here are a few suggestions for how you can help your kids do just that:

Tykes (From Three Years Old to Six Years Old)

- Model generosity by congratulating your children's friends for a job well done. Keep up with their accomplishments, too. Be the first one to give a pat on the back and a hug for playing a good game or earning an award. Show your children how to love others generously.

- Give a smile to a stranger who looks sad. We all need a smile, don't we?

- Give the gift of prayer for someone who needs God's help. Let your children see you "praying on the spot" for those who need it. We often say, "I'll pray for you." Instead, pray with them before you leave their presence.

- Give a helping hand to strangers and friends alike.

  - Open a door.

  - Offer to carry bags.

  - Give change to the person in front of you who's digging around for the right coins.

  - Don't take the closest parking place; let the person behind you have it.

- Give a word of encouragement to someone.

- Give your children two banks—one for keeping, one for giving. Teach your tykes to set aside a portion of their allowance for savings, not just savings for a future purchase, but savings to give away. When I was a child, my family had miniature tin globes that doubled as a bank for our church's global missions. Each week when I received my allowance, I dropped a coin in my piggy bank and dropped another coin in the globe.

  One Sunday morning an emergency plea was given to our congregation for one of our foreign missionaries. I raised my hand along with the grown-ups to signify I would make a pledge. That night I brought my globe and emptied it in the offering plate. I still remember how good it felt that I could help, just like the adults.

- Read your tykes stories about generous people. One of the most beloved stories in the Bible is about Jesus feeding the five thousand from a young boy's offering of five loaves and two fish. This story teaches the great principle of generosity: Jesus multiplies our offerings. When we give our best, He uses it to accomplish great things. (See Matthew 14:14–21, Mark 6:34–44, Luke 9:10–17, and John 6:1–11.)

  The story of Milton Hershey is also inspiring. He and his wife were never able to have children, but before his death Mr. Hershey founded a boarding school for children and left the bulk of his fortune to take care of the kids who would attend the school for generations to come. He lived a modest life by most standards, devoting his time and energy to building a chocolate empire that would produce the best product and take good care of its employees. *Chocolate by Hershey*, by Betty Burford, tells Mr. Hershey's life's story, from its slow beginning to its magnanimous ending.

Tweens to Teens (From Six Years Old to Nineteen Years Old)

- Have an open-door policy for your kids' friends. Don't be surprised when one or two teens prefer talking to you on a Friday night rather than hanging out with their buddies. One of the greatest gifts you can give your teenagers is to listen to their friends.

  Most Friday and Saturday nights during my sons' high school years, when the crowd left our kitchen for the game room, one teen would lag behind just to talk. On a few occasions, my sons encouraged friends to come to me with their problems. I never considered this a burden, but a privilege, because my sons counted on me to be there for their friends.

  During their college days, my sons carried on the family tradition. They helped more than one friend who needed a helping hand. Their generous hearts made them first responders to friends and strangers in need.

- Encourage your kids to give of their time to others. If your teen is an exceptional math student, encourage her to help a student who is struggling. If your teen is a natural with electronic gadgets, encourage him to offer his talents to help at church or school.

- Teach money management. Your teens won't have money to share with those in need if they don't know how to manage it. They should learn how to keep a checkbook, save, tithe, and give. Help your teens understand the blessing of money, that we are blessed to bless others.

Open hands develop open hearts. Giving to others is one of the great pleasures in life. "Give and it will be given to you. A good measure, pressed down, shaken together and running over, will be poured in your lap. For with the measure you use, it will be measured to you" (Luke 6:38).

Forgiveness and generosity reside in unselfish hearts. So does gratitude.

NURTURING GRATITUDE

Give Them Less Stuff

A wise father raising his family in an affluent section of London was concerned about his son's attitude toward their wealth. Timothy Lancaster wanted his son, Kirk, to appreciate the advantages of his upbringing, so Dad planned a trip to the country to visit relatives. He believed that if his son could experience life without all the "extras," he would be grateful for what he had.

When they arrived at the modest farm, Kirk said not a word of complaint when he discovered there were few amenities and even fewer forms of entertainment. He dashed off with his cousins to explore the countryside.

Supper was soup and salad with an apple for dessert. Kirk slept with his three cousins in the same room and awakened shortly after dawn to help out with the chores.

When they arrived home from their trip Mr. Lancaster asked Kirk how he enjoyed his visit. "It was very good, Dad!" he replied.

"Did you see how poor people can be?" his father asked.

"Yes, sir," Kirk answered. "I saw that we have a dog at home, and they have four. We have a pool in the middle of the garden, but they have a creek that has no end. We have fancy lamps in the garden, but they have stars."

When the son finished, his father was speechless.

Kirk then added, "Thanks, Dad, for showing me how poor we are!" [1]

Kirk's observation certainly took his father by surprise. His father had expected him to recognize how fortunate they were *not* to have to live like his cousins. But Kirk saw the real riches his cousins possessed in having little material wealth.

Children don't need stuff to be content, particularly if they grow up in a God-centered family. David Staal, director of Promiseland, the children's ministry at Willow Creek Community Church, gives two reasons why:

First, kids who learn a lot about God gain a healthy perspective on life. Specifically, they understand that life is not "all about me." In fact, life is all about God—which takes away a lot of pressure for individuals to impress others. Eliminate that pressure, and materialism begins to disintegrate. This God-centered perspective also opens up their hearts to appreciate the sheer wonder of all that the Lord has created and the blessing of his provisions. And second, children who regularly hear that God desires a relationship with them and freely offers his love will realize they can have what they really want—which money just can't buy.[2]

If we want to nurture gratitude in our children's hearts, we need to give them less stuff. In giving our children less, we give them more. More of the right stuff. Remember the Christmas your two-year-old opened his gifts, pushed them aside, and played with the ribbons instead? There's a lesson for all of us in that simple act of pleasure.

Tame the Greedy Monster in You

Your kids will follow your example when it comes to how much stuff they want to own. So, check the greedy monster in you before you start working on your children:

- Do you want more and more money? Is it to buy more or give more?

- Do you repair or replace when "technical" problems happen with appliances?

- Do you give something to anyone who asks? The beggar on the street? The kids in front of Wal-Mart? The Salvation Army bell ringer?

- Do you have to have the latest model car?

- Are you faithful to tithe to your local church?

- Do you own your money or does your money own you?

- What are you thankful for? (If your answer includes lots of stuff, you've got some heart work to do.)

If your answers revealed the need to tame the greedy monster in you, consider the following suggestions for how to do so:

- Be satisfied with last year's whatever. Let your children see that you don't toss things aside because they're used. They need to see that as things become old, they become precious, rather than obsolete. (Don't you want them to feel that way about you?)

- Pay as you go. Rather than pull out your plastic, teach your children by example that it's better to pay as you go, which means saving for purchases, rather than buying on credit. Help your children weigh the pros and cons of purchases. Delayed gratification often changes "I have to have it" to "I'd like to have it" to "I don't need it."

With the greedy monster tamed, you'll be more capable of implementing the next recommendation.

Unplug Those Electronics

We receive fascinating e-mails at Manners of the Heart from teachers using our curriculum materials, parents who've read our books, and children who want to ask Wilbur questions. The success stories warm our hearts and encourage us to work harder at our mission to help today's children grow up to become who God created them to be.

One such e-mail came a few weeks ago:

I heard Ms. Rigby speak last fall at my children's school. I thought she gave good information, but went too far when she recommended unplugging our house on a Saturday. The kids got electronic games for Christmas, and my husband is a sports fanatic. A month after Christmas I was so sick of everybody "tuning out" on the weekend, that I lost it and took away all the stuff and told my husband things had to change and he had to help me.

The next weekend we unplugged just like she said. I even

said no telephones! The kids hated it at first, but warmed up to the idea when my husband and I got out some old games. Then we played some card games. The day got better and better. We played games and had ice cream after lunch. We lit candles when it got dark and told stories. We've done it many times and our kids' friends even ask to come over and try it.

My kids aren't asking for new games anymore. They're not asking for much anymore. Now they complain if we watch too much television!

Sometimes, the greatest challenges have the simplest solutions, don't they?

Implement These Simple Ideas
Here are some additional ways to instill gratitude in kids:

- Don't allow your children to have something every time it's offered. In the old days, before suckers were outlawed, every time the boys and I drove through the bank, the teller offered the boys a lollipop. Rather than allowing the treat just because it was offered, I said "Thank you, but not today," on occasion. The boys learned that the lollipop was a treat, not a "right."

- Encourage the simple pleasures: Make homemade gifts for each other. Play games rather than rent a movie. Spend the night in the backyard as an adventure at home.

- Require your children to purchase their "wants" with extra money that they earn for doing chores. This not only instills gratitude, but it also builds self-respect.

- When you pray with your children, encourage them to make thanksgiving the most important part of their prayer.

In everything give thanks;
for this is the will of God in Christ Jesus concerning you.
1 THESSALONIANS 5:18 KJV

- Help your children memorize Philippians 4:8: "Finally, brothers, whatever is true, whatever is noble, whatever is right, whatever is pure, whatever is lovely, whatever is admirable—if anything is excellent or praiseworthy—think about such things."

- Require your kids to write thank-you notes. Beginning at the age of three, your children can "draw" thank-you notes. As soon as they are able, they need to write their own. A simple thank-you note from a child warms the heart of the recipient and teaches your child the importance of saying thank you.

- Try to not let a day pass by without asking your children (from toddlers to teens) to name at least two things they appreciated during the day.

- Wherever you go, point out the good you see people doing. Express your thanks to those who are serving you and teach your children to do the same. In restaurants, at the bank, at the grocery—everywhere you go, offer your gratitude for the little things people do.

Take to heart a prayer given by one of our magnanimous presidents, Harry Truman:

Oh Almighty and Everlasting God, Creator of heaven and earth and the universe: Help me to be, to think, to act what is right, because it is right. Make me truthful, honest, and honorable in all things. Make me intellectually honest for sake of right and honor and without thought of reward to me. Give me the ability to be charitable, forgiving, and patient with my fellow men—help me to understand their motives and shortcomings—even as thou understandest mine. Amen.[3]

If only we would make this our daily prayer, our children would be the most unselfish generation that ever was. It all begins with you.

YOU ARE THE EDUCATOR OF YOUR CHILDREN'S HEARTS

I had been marking the days since September. May had finally arrived, and I was more than ready for high school to end.

One morning when I came to the table for breakfast, a handsome silver goblet held my serving of milk instead of the chipped jelly jar I had used since second grade. I saw upon closer inspection that my initials and the date of my birth were carved on the smooth face of the goblet.

My, oh my, it was beautiful.

Being a typical self-focused teen, I thought, *My birth date? Where's my graduation date?*

Mother was crying while Daddy smiled. To commemorate my passage from home to "somewhere out there," Mother had convinced Daddy I was mature enough to appreciate an unusual graduation gift—a set of silver goblets, each engraved with a significant event in my life.

During the next couple of weeks, I found goblets in unexpected places: tucked in a bouquet of flowers from the grocery store the night of our senior play; on the bedside table, filled with daisies one morning; tied to my worn-out ballet shoes; and resting in my cap the morning of the baccalaureate service. By graduation day I had eighteen shimmering goblets on my dresser. A few of the moments from my life that my mother had had engraved on the goblets:

"Little Miss Vicksburg" September 19, 1957 (I was a ten-
  month-old beauty queen.)
"First school day" September 4, 1962
"Accepted Christ" February 12, 1964
"First date" October 8, 1971

Wonder how Mother had such an accurate accounting? For more than twenty years she filled "little black books" with the day-to-day activities of our family. She didn't pour her heart out in her journals, but noted with an occasional comment of her own moments in our lives that would otherwise have been forgotten. Here's a tiny sampling:

- Jill Anne rode without training wheels . . . good, but sad, too.

- Finished playhouse. Girls cried hard they were so happy. Now they'll learn to play together with happy hearts. No more fussing.

- Bought a new washing machine.

- We made it to Six Flags . . . tired. Children said thank you.

- Jill Anne learned a hard lesson today . . . hard on me. Good for her heart.

- Girls tried to stay up all night. Found them asleep on the floor by the Monopoly board. Covered them up and kissed them. (Summer slumber party.)

- Worried about a hard heart in one of my children. Prayed long today.

- Spent the day at Rocky Springs. Good day.

- Silly girls. Laughed so hard, we all cried. (I don't know what was so funny!)

Mother always said, "It's the little things that matter most." Her journals proved she truly believed it. She captured the little everyday happenings in our family that made our simple lives richly complex.

Did you notice the entries in her journal that mentioned her concern for our hearts? Page after page recounted the daily building of her children's character. Mother was, and still is, one of those mothers who wants her children to be their best. Her words, "Pretty is as pretty does" lull me to sleep many nights and echo through my heart the next morning.

Today the goblets my mother gave me are displayed on hanging shelves in my dining room. They're not worth much to guests in my home, but to me, they're priceless. As I gently remove the tarnish, I'm reminded of my mother's great love for her children. She was determined to rub away the tarnish on our hearts before they became blackened from sin. She polished and cleaned us everyday. She worried much more about our hearts than about our minds. She believed it was *her* duty to prepare us for life and *our* duty to participate in life. Mother educated our hearts, so we could educate our minds.

Children don't need a lot of things when their hearts are full of the right stuff. Your kids see into your heart. They know love when they see it. They know it when they don't see it. Your heart is eternally connected to your children's hearts. Use the influence God has given you to fill your children's hearts with forgiveness, generosity, and gratitude.

TWENTY YEARS OF PRAYER

1st year—"Father, I pray for your parenting wisdom."

2nd year—"Oh, Lord, give me patience."

3rd year—"Father, grant me the stamina to run the race set before me."

4th year—"Father, teach me your secret of firm, gentle discipline."

5th year—"Father, never let me forget this child is a gift from you to be cherished."

6th year—"Father, enable me to teach your rules, not mine."

7th year—"Lord, help me to listen, when I'm too tired to listen."

8th year—"Father, give me creativity to engage my child, not entertain."

9th year—"Oh, Lord, I make so many mistakes. Thank you that love covers a multitude of mistakes."

10th year—"Father, I pray for peace. First in my soul and then in my home."

11th year—"Father, help me to be the person you want my child to become."

12th year—"Father, search me and know my heart. Test me and know my anxious thoughts."

13th year—"Oh, Lord, I'm running on empty. I need another filling of patience."

14th year—"Father, I pray for courage to maintain boundaries."

15th year—"Father, don't let me stand in the way of your discipline."

16th year—"Father, go before my child and come behind. Surround him with your angels and keep him in your care."

17th year—"Oh, Father, help! My child wants to be an adult."

18th year—"Father, remind me every day that once upon a time I was eighteen."

19th year—"Father, keep my mouth shut and my heart open."

20th year—"Father, I pray that my adult child will stand for you in the world."

PART THREE

Rebuilding Our World

We do not need more material development;
we need more spiritual development.
We do not need more intellectual power;
we need more moral power.
We do not need more knowledge,
we need more character.
We do not need more government,
we need more culture.
We do not need more law; we need more religion.
We do not need more of the things that are seen,
We need more of the things that are unseen.

President Calvin Coolidge

CHAPTER 11

Giving Love to Your Community

CHRISTMAS OFFICIALLY BEGINS in Baton Rouge the first Friday night of December. Majestic live oaks and mounds of azaleas covered in tiny white lights line North Boulevard, giving the illusion of glistening snow.

First Presbyterian Church stands proudly alongside other historic buildings on the promenade. Ten years ago, members of our congregation were hanging fresh greenery on the massive sanctuary doors when the sound of bells rang in the distance. We stopped our work to watch runners with jingle bells tied to their shoelaces pass by. The annual Jingle Bell Run was under way.

We had timed our celebration so we could stand on the front steps and carol as the jingle bell runners passed by. Much to our surprise and delight, a number of the participants came around after their race to say thank you. Several commented they hadn't heard Christmas carols in years. We were pleased they were touched, but we knew we had to do more. The time had come for the return of "Silent Night," our church's live nativity presentation.

As we prepared for this presentation to our community, old and young alike found ways to offer themselves in service. Women volunteered to tackle the difficult costumes while men offered to grow beards in order to become Wise Men and shepherds. Two brave young women agreed to share duties as the angel who would hover more than twenty feet above the ground.

A gentleman who had participated in the live nativity as a child stepped forward to build the structure from forty-year-old plans. He even convinced a group of men to give up Friday-after-Thanksgiving-football in order to construct the humble stable. Finally everything was ready, and we suspended a star in the sky to illuminate the scene.

The streetlights were dimmed at our corner so that the soft glow of the holy star could shine its light on the manger. Goats, sheep, and livestock grazed near the stable, just as they had that special night two thousand years ago. Mary and Joseph settled in with baby Jesus. Shepherds waited close by for the star to signal their journey; the Wise Men prepared their gifts for the King.

All the while, we could hear loud music from the other end of the street, where vendors were selling Christmas cheer and good food, and I got an idea. "Wait, wait!" I shouted, waving my arms like an out-of-control director. "Let's send Mary and Joseph down the boulevard, looking for a place to stay."

The thought of Mary and Joseph meandering through the rowdy crowd sent HolyGhostbumps up my spine. Without hesitation, Joseph assisted Mary as she mounted the donkey for a ride back to the future. A few of us followed to watch the reactions of folks who might be surprised by such a sight.

Beer flowed freely while the band rocked 'round the Christmas tree as Mary rode sidesaddle and Joseph led the way, wandering through the "real" world without announcement or fanfare.

But even without introduction, folks recognized the famous couple. Conversations stopped. Heads turned. The music fell silent. Merriment became reverence.

For a few brief moments, the world stood still.

Joseph led Mary back down the boulevard, to the stable, where a different crowd had gathered. Elderly folks sat in heated vans, peering through the windows. School-age children waited to see the animals and a special baby. Families had gathered around the crèche to be reminded of the reason for the season.

As the sounds of "Silent Night" filled the air, older children ran to the animals, while the younger ones ran past the livestock to see baby Jesus. A charming young girl climbed into Mary's lap. In her hand was a well-loved stuffed frog with long scraggly legs. No doubt, wherever this little girl went the little frog went with her.

The adoring child looked into Mary's eyes and asked if she could talk to Jesus. Mary said, "Yes, my child. Jesus came for you." That precious child leaned forward, lifting the wrap from Jesus's face to gently kiss his forehead and whisper, "I love you, *too*, Jesus."

Not, I love you—but I love you, *too*.

Sliding from Mary's lap, she turned to walk away, but stopped, looked back at Jesus, and placed her most prized possession, the frog with scraggly legs, in the manger next to Jesus.

Never had any of us witnessed such a pure acceptance of the Gospel. Not only did this little girl understand God's invitation, but she had received the Good News by responding with love to the One who first loved her. In turn, she gave her best to Jesus because He gave His best for her.

BLESSED TO BE A BLESSING

I couldn't write this book about raising self-less children without challenging you to begin to change our self-absorbed world. How can any of us change our communities? By leading them to the manger. When we love our communities *for* Christ, our communities will be drawn *to*

Christ. It means blessing others from the rich blessings God has given us. God made this clear in the opening chapters of His Word.

> The Lord had said to Abram, "Leave your country, your people and your father's household and go to the land I will show you. I will make you into a great nation and *I will bless you; I will make your name great, and you will be a blessing.* I will bless those who bless you, and whoever curses you I will curse; *and all peoples on earth will be blessed through you."* (Genesis 12:1–3, emphasis added)

In other words, God told Abram, "I will bless you, so that you will be a blessing." God's plan from the beginning was to bless those who love Him so that they can bless others on His behalf. We, too, are blessed to be blessings to others.

However, if we Christians did a better job of living the Gospel, we wouldn't have to spend so much time and effort telling the Gospel. If we did a better job as Christ's ambassadors, others would want what we have. They would run to us for the answers we've found. But too often, we live selfish lives; we love money while we use people and squabble among ourselves. Rather than standing out as different, we look and act much like everyone else. Rather than asking God to bless those around us, we ask Him to bless us.

But there are families and churches that are living the Gospel in their communities.

> When we love our communities *for* Christ,
> our communities will be drawn *to* Christ.
> WISE OLD WILBUR

Be inspired by the following true stories of folks who reach out in unique ways to love and serve their communities, which extend well beyond the boundaries of home and church. They include neighborhoods, schools, cities, and the surrounding areas. I hope their example motivates you to come up with ways that you, too, can involve your family in loving your community.

Host a Neighborhood Bible Club

The Harris family of Wheaton, Illinois, joined with other families in their church to host Neighborhood Bible Clubs during the summer. They believed kids who wouldn't attend a Vacation Bible School in a church might be more likely to come to a neighborhood event. Sure enough, the first summer they had thirty kids. This number grew to near one hundred in later years.

Shawna Harris Gose, who was blessed to have grown up in the Harris family, told me this about the experience:

> We hosted a club for ten to eleven years, starting from the time I was in fourth grade to my sophomore year of college. I was able to be a "kid helper" the first couple years while older kids in our neighborhood helped with the younger kids. From seventh grade through college, my sisters and I helped lead a small group. There were also moms in the community and from our church who helped keep things organized. Teams competed with each other by reciting verses, answering questions at the end of story time, bringing friends to the club, and by being good and kind and paying attention. At the end, the team with the most peanuts were the winners!
>
> The first day of the club we had a "fun fare" with different booths and prizes. The last day was "water day" when the kids wore swimsuits and played water games for an hour. We even threw water balloons!

Shawna said children came to Christ, moms made new friendships, and neighbors saw the love of Christ in action.

TIPS FOR HOSTING A NEIGHBORHOOD BIBLE CLUB

The Neighborhood Club was held Monday through Friday from nine to noon for one week of the summer in different families' homes. A typical schedule:

1. Kids would sign in in the morning and find their team in the backyard.

2. The first fifteen minutes would consist of kids reciting their memorized verse of the day to team leaders. (All verses were learned by song the day before.) Leaders would distribute peanuts for attendance and verse recitation.

3. All the teams came together for song time.

4. Some teams would stay together for story time, while the rest rotated from crafts to snacks.

5. Everyone came together again for a couple more songs and closing. The Harris's church provided the theme, curriculum, crafts, music, material for fun-fare, and T-shirts for the kids.

Start a "We Care" Team for Homeless Shelters

During the month of May, the Williams family sends out invitations to a "We Care" party held at the end of summer. Each family that receives an invitation is asked to become a member of the "We Care" team by collecting shampoo, lotion, sewing kits, and coffee packets during the summer that will be put into care packets for the homeless. (If you stay in hotels when you travel, you can collect the complementary bottles and packages of these items that are placed in your room each day.)

The day of the "We Care" party, the Williamses set up tables for the families to sort and package the collected items in Ziploc bags for distribution. The children write out scriptures that are included in each bag. Toothbrushes, toothpaste, and combs are added to complete the packages, which are then distributed to homeless shelters across the city.

The Williamses also keep fast-food coupons in their car for their children to give anyone who asks for help. This is a family who cares!

> And whatever you do, whether in word or deed,
> do it all in the name of the Lord Jesus,
> giving thanks to God the Father through him.
>
> Colossians 3:17

Cheerful Voices for "Grandfriends"

Martha began encouraging her elementary-school-age children to respect the elderly by taking her kids on regular visits to shut-ins. Her children would draw pictures, make cookies, and create special homemade gifts for their "grandfriends."

On one such visit, her kids learned that their new "grandfriend," Mrs. Preston, was blind. She was a sweet lady with a gentle spirit, and she deeply appreciated their visit. When they were leaving she said, "Thank you for coming to see me. I loved hearing your cheerful voices." On the way home, one of the children asked their mom if there was something special they could do for Mrs. Preston. Martha had the perfect idea.

Each of the children recorded a psalm on tape for their "grandfriend" to listen to between visits. In a few months they had recorded the entire book of Psalms! Martha starting making copies of the recordings to distribute to other nursing home residents. Her two older children, now college students, continue the outreach by recording books for shut-in residents in their college town.

Share Your Passion

The YMCA has been Dean Cooper's home away from home for the last two years. He recognized that his membership gave him an opportunity to help others strengthen their spirits by studying God's Word.

A passionate master teacher of the Bethel Bible Series, a two-year interdenominational study of Scripture, Dean approached the leadership of the Y with the offer to teach weekly sessions. They enthusiastically welcomed his idea and Bethel at the Y began. Trained volunteer instructors lead the sessions for participants who are finding more than they bargained for at their local YMCA.

Your passion may be sewing, cooking, building models, soap making, woodworking, or any number of interesting pastimes. Offer to teach a class at your local Y or community center, not for pay, but for the satisfaction of sharing your passion with others. Many of the hobbies of yesteryear aren't being taught to the next generation.

Organize an Old-Fashioned Christmas Caroling

For many years friends gathered at the Treppendahls' home each December for cocoa and sweet treats before strolling down the streets, singing a mixture of traditional and sacred carols to entertain the neighbors. To conclude the evening, everyone returned to the Treppendahls' home for a time of prayer and blessing for the New Year.

A couple of additional ideas to enhance your caroling experience:

- Help the children make songbooks for everyone, including the people whose homes they visit.

- Include a copy of the Christmas story from Luke 2.

MAKING THE MOST OF
FAMILY VOLUNTEER TIME

In *Growing Compassionate Kids,* author Jan Johnson offers these valuable suggestions:

1. Find activities that are within the capabilities of all family members, especially if you're including preschoolers or grandparents. Or you may want to join another family in a project to make it more fun. How a family chooses to serve together will be as different as families themselves.

2. Pray with your children for the people you're going to serve. You could do that several times at a meal or bedtime before and after you serve. Let your kids see that your relationship with God motivates you to love others.

3. When you visit a nursing home, homeless shelter, or soup kitchen, develop friendships. We don't serve to simply "do good." When we served dinner at a street mission, we always carved out time for our kids to play with kids from the mission's neighborhood.[1]

Say Thanks to Those Who Bless Your Family
The Mortons are a family that loves to give. One year Pat, a thoughtful ninth-grader, surprised the school guards, cafeteria workers, and jani-

torial staff at her school with a thank you for their hard work. She expressed her appreciation for their role in making her school a great place to learn with handwritten notes and a gift certificate for ice cream at the local creamery.

The school was so touched by Pat's kindness, when Christmas rolled around they decided to ask each class to adopt a support staff member as their way of saying thank you as a school family.

More money won't solve the problems in our communities. More technology won't fill the minds of kids with empty hearts. The solution to this problem is love. It *is* that simple. Scripture gives us the simple answer to our most difficult problems: "Dear children, Let us not love with words or tongue but with actions and in truth"(1 John 3:18).

HELPING THE NEXT GENERATION IN OUR COMMUNITIES

I was reminded of the truth of 1 John 3:18 (above) a few years ago when I was speaking to a group of high school students in an inner-city school.

Three hundred fifty pairs of eyes stared at me as I asked, "Which do you want to be? Number one or the best?" Enthusiastic voices filled with great conviction responded from across the room, "Number one, number one!"

"Number one, huh?" I replied. "I hope to convince you otherwise."

Much of what they heard from me that day ran counter to the messages they were receiving at home and in school. I talked about the difference between striving to be number one and striving to be the best. If you strive to be number one, you'll compete with others. If you strive to be the best, you'll only compete with yourself. If you strive to be number one, you'll give up when someone beats you. If you strive to be the best, you'll persevere until you reach your goal.

I talked about rectifying your mistakes rather than concealing them. I talked about the need for significance being greater than the need for success. I encouraged having old-fashioned manners—putting the needs of others ahead of your own wants.

To close our time together, I gave the students this manners test. I said, "Last week someone special made your all-time favorite cookies. I don't mean slice-and-bake or add-water-to-the-mix cookies. I mean, real, made-from-scratch cookies. This was the first batch of homemade cookies you've had in more than a year."

I stopped here and asked their favorite cookie. Almost in unison they said chocolate chip, to which I made the offhand remark, "I make killer chocolate chip cookies."

I continued, "A friend comes by to see you. There are only two cookies left on the plate . . . a nice, big cookie and a small cookie that must have been the last bit of dough. Your friend is eying those cookies. What will you do? Will you offer your friend the big cookie or the little cookie?"

Here are a few of their responses:

- "I'd give 'em the little cookie, of course. I don't have to give either, they both belong to me."

- "I'd give 'em the little cookie and a piece of the big cookie, so my friend knows who's boss."

- "I know you want me to say that I'd give 'em the big cookie, but hey, I gotta' take care of myself first."

Why were these high schoolers' answers so self-absorbed? Because they didn't know they're loved. No one has loved them enough to take them to the window.

Let me prove my point. After the manners test, a young man called out, "Heeeey, Miss Jill, why did you come to our school? I mean, why do you bother? What's up with you anyway?"

Why do I do what I do? I thought. *Why do I try so hard to reach kids? Why did I come here today? What's up with me?* The answer came in an epiphany of epic proportion. I walked to the back of the cafeteria, took hold of the young man's shoulders, and said, "Because I love you. That's why I'm here." Words cannot describe his stunned expression. "Do you believe me?" I prodded.

After a moment of thought, he replied, "'I *belieeeeeeeeve* I do."

I hugged him and he hugged me back.

As I moved back to the front of the room, I swung my arms open and said, "I love you, all of you. I can say it and mean it. I love you and want to help you become all you're meant to be!"

As if on cue, the bell rang. Class dismissed.

An amazing thing happened as I stood in the corridor as the kids filed out. They started passing by saying, "Hey, I love you, too." One after another after another. One of the boys asked about my "killer" cookies. I was so overjoyed that I told him I'd bake a batch of cookies—for all of them!

Manners of the Heart headquarters became a cookie factory for the next two days. We all pitched in to bake, bag, and deliver seven hundred cookies. The next week, a young man left a manila envelope and a rolled banner on the front desk of our office, without saying a word. We unrolled the banner to find words of thanks written by the high schoolers to the "cookie lady." We opened the envelope to find more than two hundred letters from students. I was in tears before I could finish the first one. It took a couple of days and a box of Kleenex to read through them all.

One particular letter resonated in my soul because the message of the young man who penned the words offered the real answers for the kids in our communities:

Dear Ms. Jill,

I am writing this letter to you because I want to thank you so much for taking your time and coming to speak to our school. This means a lot to me because I know that someone in this world actually loves and cares about me. That day

214

started off a little rough for me, but when I heard you speak and sing that most wonderful song, I just had to get over my bad day. To see how much energy and how happy you were made me realize that being mad is not going to get me anywhere. All it leaves is a very negative attitude behind it. After I saw you, my day was enlightened. You were so lovable. The speech you gave was beyond wonderful. It taught me a lot because I was not a very big manners person. I was always rude, then I had to realize that I had to treat others the way I want to be treated. You were the person that opened my eyes up to that, and I really do thank you. You inspired me so much, you changed my life. I also want to thank you for the cookies, they were extremely good. Another thing I like about you is that you are a person of your word, when you say you are going to do something, you do it and do it on time. I like that in a person. No one else I know does that.

Love,
Lee

This young man's note identified what we need to do to help the next generation in our communities become selfless givers rather than selfish takers:

1. *Do what we say we are going to do.* We're responsible for raising the bar of integrity before the young people of today. We're responsible for setting the example. Lee doesn't have adults in his life that do what they say they're going to do. How can we expect the children in our neighborhoods and cities to become honest, trustworthy citizens, if they never encounter adults who promise to do good and then do it? No wonder schools are wrestling with 90 percent of students cheating on course work.

2. *Respect others as we want to be respected.* Scripture doesn't give us any ifs, ands, buts, or maybes when it comes to God's commands. Lee understood for the first time how much better life can be when you treat others with respect, because he experienced respect that day.

> Leave every soul the braver and happier
> for having met you. For children or youth,
> middle or old age, for sorrow, for sin,
> for all you may encounter in others,
> This should be your attitude. *Love and Laugh.*
> A. J. RUSSELL, *GOD CALLING*

3. *Be lovable.* Even grizzly bears can choose to be teddy bears. Wouldn't you use the word *lovable* to describe Jesus? He gently touched those in need, He wept with those who wept, He spoke the truth in love. He enjoyed life because He came to love.

As far as we know, Jesus was never one to complain. It got a little rough near the end of His life on earth, but even then, He gave His distress back to the Father and willingly went to the cross. We have to have the right attitude about life if we want the children of the next generation to have the right attitude. If we're complainers, they're going to complain. If we find good in every situation, they'll learn to look for good in the bad.

I'm often asked by high school students where my enthusiasm comes from. This is the million-dollar question I hope for, because regardless of the setting, I'm free to share the truth. I usually ask if anyone was awake at four o'clock that morning with me. I share how much the early morning means to me because it's easier to "hear" God's directions for my day when the rest of the world is still quiet. I tell them that God has a plan for every day, and how much richer life is when I'm following His directions rather than my own. Often kids linger after, wanting to know more about hearing God's voice. These opportunities for witness can't happen unless we love our communities beyond the walls of our homes.

4. *Give your time.* Time is love without words. We all have rough days, but for some kids a rough day means they were beaten by a drunken parent or spent the day hungry because there wasn't any food in the house. When you take an hour out of your rough day to spend time with a child who's having a rough day, you'll turn the day around for both of you.

This bears repeating: *Kids can't love others until they know they're loved.* They can't give to others, until they know they're loved. You see, loving yourself doesn't break your selfish heart. That only happens when you know someone loves you. In the high school that day, some students encountered someone who loved them just because she loved them. They didn't have to earn that love and they couldn't lose that love. It wasn't contingent upon worthiness but upon the giver's grace. That's the love that transforms.

Paul explains Jesus's teaching on the importance of fulfilling God's law through love:

Love other people as well as you do yourself. You can't go wrong when you love others. When you add up everything in the law code, the sum total is love. (Romans 13:8 MSG)

This is the love our communities need.

This is the love that breaks through self-absorbed hearts, breaks down self-constructed walls, and breaks apart self-inflated egos.

CHAPTER 12

Making a Difference in the World

Remember when . . .
Little girls looked like little girls?
Children were considered a blessing?
Saturday was family day?
A love song was about true love?
Lucy and Desi Arnaz slept in twin beds?
Families ate supper together?
We were one nation under God?

Today . . .
Little girls look more like twenty-somethings than little girls.
Children are often considered a curse.
Saturday is every person for himself or herself.
A love song . . . ? I don't think so.
Meredith Grey sleeps in bed with multiple men.
Most families don't eat together.
We're one nation under "none."

Remember when . . .
A young boy sneaked a peek at women's lingerie
in the Sears Roebuck catalog?
Stores were closed on Sunday?
Displays of public affection were considered in poor taste?
Public schools were the center of our communities?
There were only three choices of tennis shoes?
The divorce rate was 10 percent?
Bare legs were scandalous?

Today . . .
A young boy sees sexy lingerie in the Victoria's Secret window.
Even construction workers work on Sunday.
There's sex in the city, sex in the country, sex in the schools.
Public schools are failing and closing.
There are hundreds of brands of tennis shoes.
The divorce rate is 52 percent.
Panty hose are now passé.

Remember when . . .
The only television in the house was the
console in the living room?
Groceries were taken to your car by a nice young man?
The Cleavers were our favorite television family?
The president was referred to as Mr. President?
Monopoly was the number-one game?
Darn was a curse word?
Children obeyed their parents?
First came love, then came marriage,
then came Mom and Dad with a baby carriage?

Today . . .

Sixty-six percent of U.S. homes have
three or more televisions.[1]
Bag your own groceries and carry them, too.
The Osbournes are the family of choice.
The president is called by his first name.
Grand Theft Auto is the second most
popular game on PlayStation.[2]
Two-year-olds use *darn.*
Parents obey their children.
There's no love, no marriage, and often, no dad.

Has our country progressed or regressed? Are we better off today than forty years ago? Are we less selfish or more selfish? Are we happier than we were yesteryear?

We can't answer those questions without taking into account where we've been and where we are now. The great value of history is to guide the future.

In 1776, The Declaration of Independence stated that we have a right to pursue happiness. To be specific, it says "all men are created equal, that they are endowed by their Creator with certain unalienable Rights, that among these are Life, Liberty and the pursuit of Happiness." We agreed and began the pursuit of happiness in our personal, business, and social lives.

Our understanding of how to pursue happiness has changed over the years. The first American board game, the "Mansion of Happiness," was produced in 1843 by the W. & S. B. Ives Company, depicting real-life situations in which good deeds led children and their playing pieces down the path to "eternal happiness."[3] As a follow-up to the great success of the Ives game, Milton Bradley created "The Checkered Game of Life" in 1860, which rewarded good deeds and punished bad ones.[4]

But along the way we turned the pursuit of happiness into a quest for personal wealth and power. President Theodore Roosevelt tried to tell us we were pursuing the wrong things when he warned, "The things that will destroy America are prosperity at any price, peace at any price, safety first instead of duty first, the love of soft living and the get rich quick theory of life."[5]

We disagreed and continued to seek pleasure in entertainment, empire building, and easy living.

Since the 1960s we have taken the pursuit of happiness to new levels. Carl Rogers told us we needed self-esteem to be happy. Sounded like a good thing, so we turned away from the windows that looked out into the world and became mesmerized by the images we found in our own mirrors. The pursuit of happiness became, "It's all about me." As our children came along, we presented them with sterling-silver mirrors, telling them, "It's all about you." Take a glance back at chapter 2 to be reminded just how seriously we have taken this pursuit.

Our self-absorption has led to an obsession with personal profit rather than concern for the common good. We've become so lost in our mirrors that we've lost sight of the fact that we are citizens of a world that needs our help.[6]

The highest glory of the American Revolution was this:
that it connected, in one indissoluble bond, the principles
of civil government with the principles of Christianity.
JOHN QUINCY ADAMS

We, the citizens of this country, are supposed to be in charge of running it—not Washington, special interest groups, rich corporations, or Hollywood billionaires. We are the boss of our elected officials at all levels of government—local, state, and national. They work for us. They do not elect themselves; we elect them, either by voting or staying away from the polls. Sad to say, many of us are giving away our freedoms by our lack of involvement. It's as much our lack of interest as it is their shortsightedness that allows our elected officials to believe we are meant to follow their lead, rather than the other way around.

> The government is us; we are the government, you and I.
> THEODORE ROOSEVELT

We're paying a hefty price for our lack of interest in participating in the political process. One of our state senators reminds his constituents at every opportunity he is given that it only takes five phone calls, e-mails, or letters to persuade your representative in government to vote according to your wishes. Yes, that's right, just five contacts on any given bill. He typically receives no calls from votes on the "family friendly" side of issues. With almost unfailing commitment, he receives at least two calls from those seeking to diminish the strength of the family.[7]

No one is taking away our rights; *we're not using them.* Remember "*of* the people, *by* the people, and *for* the people?" With great freedom and privilege comes even greater responsibility to serve our country and our fellow citizens.

CALLED TO SERVE

During the writing of this book I was called to jury duty for the first time in my fifty years of citizenry. When I mentioned to others that I was called to serve, I heard, "Honey, you can find a way to get out of it. I did." or "Don't worry, you can call the courthouse to be excused for personal reasons." *Personal reasons? What personal reasons?* I thought.

For those of you who have served your community in this way, you'll understand that I was the odd-woman-out in my enthusiasm the Monday morning I reported for duty. I was ready, willing, and looking forward to serving. The two hundred or so fellow citizens that were crammed into the stately room of our old state capitol didn't seem to share my eagerness, except for one older gentleman.

Our jury trainer reminded those over seventy they could excuse themselves from serving because they had earned the right to step aside by virtue of their age. Two women jumped to their feet with great delight and were applauded as they signed out. I couldn't discern if folks were applauding their age or that they had escaped jury duty. The trainer scanned the room, pausing to fix her eyes on a gentleman, much older than seventy, as if to ask without words, "What about you, sir?" He returned the gesture with a smile and said, "I'm honored to serve, ma'am," in a baritone voice that echoed across the room.

Through the words of a humble servant, we were all put to shame. Following his comment I looked around the room, looking for the reactions of my fellow jurists to this dear man's sense of civic responsibility. Some nodded with approval. Others were stunned. Some of us were deeply touched at the realization of how far we've strayed from that "one for all and all for one" stance that helped to found and build our country. This gentleman forced us to acknowledge that too often today we're only interested in "what's in it for me" rather than "what can I do to help?"

Gazing across the room, I saw diverse skin tones, ranging from darkest ebony to palest ivory and every shade between. Some had furrowed brows and sullen stares. *Are they carrying heavy burdens?* I wondered. Those with smug expressions sat shoulder to shoulder with humble folks. Finely dressed women in designer suits sat next to field hands in tattered shirts. Young "punks" rubbed elbows with austere businessmen. Individuals accustomed to giving orders waited with the rest of us to receive orders.

In the hallowed halls of justice, all of our differences came together to make us one. One body with one soul as citizens of our city and citizens of our country. My heart burst with pride. For all the difficulties, disappointments, and disgusts we deal with in our government and each other, we still reside in a country that offers us the greatest freedom of any country on earth.

As the humble gentleman reminded us, with this great freedom comes great responsibility. He was no longer required to serve, but he chose to serve.

He understood the privilege of duty. He was not lost in his mirror. He lived at the window, recognizing his responsibility to serve others because he had a role to play in our democratic republic.

We *must* join this selfless gentleman by becoming responsible citizens—which means answering the call to jury duty, being informed voters in our elections, helping organizations that protect our values, and setting an example before our children of caring enough about their future to be involved citizens.

THE COST OF INACTION

If we aren't responsible citizens, we're failing to teach our children how to make a difference in our self-absorbed world for the cause of Christ. It's one thing to be a Christian; it's another thing to be a Christian in the world. Jesus wasn't afraid to be politically incorrect. And we shouldn't be either.

Our country is drowning in political correctness. We applaud the disgusting in the name of tolerance. We berate the virtuous in the name of tolerance. Seems happiness isn't the only term we've redefined to suit our selfishness. *Tolerance* has been retermed to mean "anything goes but goodness." And who's suffering in the name of tolerance? Our children.

It isn't that the world has taken our children—
we've given the world to our children.
Wise Old Wilbur

225

If you're not convinced you *must* get involved for the sake of your children, perhaps reading a few words from someone who is bent on pushing his self-absorbed political views on our children will convince you:

> The reasons my films have been, I think, popular amongst teenagers is because I'm, like, an adult your dad's age, but I'm telling you to stick it to the man! I want young people to rebel. I want them to break the rules, to not just do what they're told. . . . I've always been happy in the past when teenagers have downloaded pirated copies of my movies, because my movies to this point have always been R-rated. Teenagers should be able to see my movies, and they haven't been able to, so they're downloading them and they're sharing them, and I think that's great. . . . At 17 you go, "That Michael Moore must be cool, because Mom and Dad think that he sucks." So the more parents that are watching Fox News and saying, "Don't listen to that Michael Moore," I think it's just code to their teenagers to maybe pay attention to some of the things I'm saying. . . . So I want young people to come to my movie and to go, "Yeah, yeah! Go Mike! F—— 'em up."
> —MICHAEL MOORE, producer of such propaganda movies as *Fahrenheit 9/11* and *Sicko,* in an interview on MTV[8]

We're a country gone wild. We shouldn't be surprised; we've been told this was coming:

> Don't be naïve. There are difficult times ahead . . . people are going to be self-absorbed, money-hungry, self-promoting, stuck-up, profane, contemptuous of parents, crude, coarse, dog-eat-dog, unbending, slanderers, impulsively wild, savage, cynical, treacherous, ruthless, bloated windbags, addicted to

lust, and allergic to God. They'll make a show of religion, but behind the scenes they're animals. Stay clear of these people. (2 Timothy 3:1–9 MSG)

So what can we do about it?

GET INVOLVED IN TANGIBLE WAYS

Look at the verses that follow:

> You are the salt of the earth. But if the salt loses its saltiness, how can it be made salty again? It is no longer good for anything, except to be thrown out and trampled by men. You are the light of the world. A city on a hill cannot be hidden. Neither do people light a lamp and put it under a bowl. Instead they put it on its stand, and it gives light to everyone in the house. In the same way, let your light shine before men, that they may see your good deeds and praise your Father in heaven. (Matthew 5:13–16)

We must take up the fight for truth in the cultural war. Public schools are teaching humanism. The media saturates us with negative news and slanted presentations of the facts. The entertainment industry cranks out poison for our children's minds and hearts to soak up. We must stand up, stand out, and be counted. We're losing by default, not because the opposition is too much for us, but because we're not engaged.

But you can change this, and make a difference in our self-absorbed world—and influence your children to do the same. Here are some suggestions to get you started:

- *Offer your home for community meetings.* This is a wonderful opportunity for your children to see the way organizations function and to begin developing a desire to be involved and take responsibility in their community one day. Your kids can help by setting up tables and chairs, greeting guests as they arrive, serving refreshments.

- *Work a political campaign.* Volunteer to distribute flyers. Canvass neighborhoods.

- *Be an informed voter.*

  - To register to vote, visit: www.ivotevalues.com.

  - Subscribe to a few online sites that send daily updates out of Washington and around the country to keep you abreast of legislation.

  - To compare the Democratic and Republican platforms on four biblical issues, visit: www.wallbuilders.com/resources/misc/Platforms.pdf.

  - To track federal legislation and learn how your congressman and senators voted, visit: www.thomas.gov.

  - The following organizations provide nonpartisan information about candidates and voting:

    - *Project Vote Smart* at www.vote-smart.org

    - *On the Issues* at www.ontheissues.org

    - *iVoteValues* at www.ivotevalues.com

    - *American Center for Law and Justice* at www.aclj.org

- *Check with your child's school to be certain they're reciting the Pledge of Allegiance every morning.* North Carolina recently passed a bill requiring schools to recite the pledge because so many were neglecting their responsibility to teach our children to respect our country.

- *Make a phone call or send an e-mail when a piece of legislation that could harm the family comes along—locally and nationally.*

- *Join one of the state family policy councils.* These organizations are the eyes and ears in your state. They work to persuasively present biblical principles in the centers of influence on issues affecting the family. (For a complete listing, see Appendix B.)

- *Take your children with you to the polls.* Explain the process to your children and why it's important to vote.

- *Consider running for your local school board.* Our public school system is greatly in need of sound leadership.

> A politician thinks of the next election;
> A statesman of the next generation.
> J. F. CLARKE

- *Talk to the manager of your local mall about the indecent and inappropriate displays in storefronts.* A couple of years ago, concerned parents became enraged at the pornographic photographs in the windows of Abercrombie & Fitch. Banding together, they were able to bring pressure to have the photos removed. Victoria's Secret is another mall store that crosses the line of decency in its mannequin displays. Phone calls and e-mails to the mall managers and owners make a difference. (For a listing of the companies that own the majority of malls in our country, see Appendix C.)

- *Write letters to the editor of your local paper about issues that concern you in your community.* Encourage your children to write a letter about troubles they see in their schools and communities.

- *Write letters to elected officials.* Tell your representatives exactly what you are thinking. For best results, write from the heart, and try a personalized letter, instead of a form letter. Contacting your representative is easy. Visit www.house.gov for contact info.

- *Attend town hall meetings, and let your local representatives know how you feel.* Need a new traffic light to help reduce speeding in your neighborhood? Tired of your public school's lack of funding? Find out when city hall has its monthly meetings, and attend. The floor opens up for new business, and you can make your opinion known.

- *Encourage your family to support global humanitarian efforts:*

  - *Compassion International* is a tax-deductible organization that exists as an advocate for children in order to release them from their spiritual, economic, social, and physical poverty and to enable them to become responsible and fulfilled Christian adults. Visit their website at www .compassion.com

  - *AmeriCares* is an international humanitarian relief organization that provides medicine, medical supplies, and other aid to individuals in need around the world. Families can create healthy kid kits that contain one toothbrush, hairbrush, bar of soap, face cloth, and small toy that are distributed to children in third world countries. Visit their website at www.americares.org

- *Contact the following pro-family organizations for how you can make a difference:*

  - The *American Family Association* was started as a Christian organization in order to help protect traditional American values. Visit their website at www.afa.net

- *One Million Moms* is an online community of mothers aimed at stopping the exploitation of our children, especially by the entertainment media. Visit their website at www.onemillionmoms.com

- *One Million Dads* is an online community of fathers aimed at stopping the exploitation of our children, especially by the entertainment media. Visit their website at www.onemilliondads.com

- *The Family Research Council* formulates public policy that values human life and upholds the institutions of marriage and the family. Visit their website at www.frc.org

- *Focus on the Family* has a vision to redeem families, communities, and societies worldwide through Christ and holds firm beliefs about both the Christian faith and the importance of the family. Visit their website at www.focusonthefamily.com

- *The Eagle Forum* has a mission to enable conservative and profamily men and women to participate in the process of self-government and public policy making. Visit their website at www.eagleforum.org

- *The National Right to Life Committee* was established in response to the U.S. legalization of human abortion and works to protect human life from the time of conception. Visit their website at www.nrlc.org

- *Christian Coalition of America* is a conservative organization offering people of faith the opportunity to be actively involved in shaping their government. Visit their website at www.cc.org

- *The Catholic Answers Action* provides voter guides and candidate guides to encourage Catholics to vote in a way

reflecting their faith. Visit their website at www.caaction
.com

- *WallBuilders* is an organization dedicated to presenting
America's forgotten history and heroes, with an emphasis
on the moral, religious, and constitutional foundation on
which America was built. Visit their website at www.wall
builders.com

He who pursues righteousness and love
finds life, prosperity and honor.
PROVERBS 21:21

FIGHTING FOR OUR COUNTRY AND OUR CHILDREN

If you had told me I would be thankful for an unexpected four-hour
delay in the Dallas airport I would have said, "Not in this lifetime." As
it turned out, I would have welcomed an additional four-hour delay
after an encounter I had with a young soldier returning home from
Iraq.

He asked if he could take the seat next to mine. I was more than
happy for the opportunity to say thank you for his service. Since 9/11
I've made it a habit to say "thank you" whenever I meet someone in
uniform. I want our soldiers to know I support their dedication to our
country and deeply appreciate their willingness to protect the rest of
us. I want them to know their service is not taken for granted.

As we began talking, he shared his days as a rebellious teenager
who found himself faced with an ultimatum from his parents—shape
up or ship out. He opted to "teach them a lesson" and ship out.

It will come as no surprise that rather than teaching his parents a
lesson, he was the one who learned a lesson. Rather than hating his
parents for their challenge, he now thanks them for it. He told me, "I
was a spoiled brat before I entered the service. The most important

person in my world was me. I found out in a hurry how unimportant my wants were, compared to the needs of our country."

At the time we spoke, this young man was in the middle of his third term of duty in as many years. He was headed home for a two-week furlough before returning for another seven months of active duty.

As he shared stories of the difficult necessity of war, I asked, "What do you think about in the midst of combat?"

"My wife and kids, my parents, my sister, my little brother, the guy next to me . . ." he replied. "I guarantee . . . most of the guys fighting are thinking about the same things. We worry about protecting our country."

"What about your personal safety?" I followed up.

Without hesitation, he said, "The only reason I worry about my safety is because if I die, that's one less guy fighting. I worry more about failing than dying."

With that, his flight was called. I shook his hand with all the passion I could muster as I wiped a tear. I hated to see him walk away, but I was so honored to have been in his presence.

What a lesson for all of us. We're fighting a cultural war. We're up against formidable opponents who seem to possess an unlimited arsenal of money and influence. If we don't do our part to make our country less self-absorbed, our country will fail. We can't complain if we wake up one day and find ourselves living in a land that's no longer the United States, land of the free and home of the brave. We must put down our mirrors, leave the mall, hide the remote control, get off the golf course, and get to work for the good of our country and the sake of our children.

TWENTY YEARS OF SCRIPTURE

1st year—"The fear of the Lord is the beginning of wisdom; all who follow his precepts have good understanding." (Psalm 111:10)

2nd year—"And do everything with love." (1 Corinthians 16:14)

3rd year—"Better a patient man than a warrior, a man who controls his temper than one who takes a city." (Proverbs 16:32)

4th year—"Be kind and compassionate to one another, tenderhearted, and forgiving each other, just as in Christ, God forgave you." (Ephesians 4:32)

5th year—"We will tell the next generation the praiseworthy deeds of the Lord, his power, and the wonders he has done." (Psalm 78:4)

6th year—"The goal of this command is love, which comes from a pure heart and a good conscience and a sincere faith." (1 Timothy 1:5)

7th year—"How good and pleasant it is when brothers live together in unity!" (Psalm 133:1)

8th year—"The wise in heart are called discerning, and pleasant words promote instruction." (Proverbs 16:21)

9th year—"Clothe yourselves with compassion, kindness, humility, gentleness and patience." (Colossians 3:12)

10th year—"Fathers, do not exasperate your children; instead bring them up in the training and instruction of the Lord." (Ephesians 6:4)

11th year—"Let the peace of Christ rule in your hearts . . . and be thankful. Let the word of Christ dwell in you richly as you teach and admonish one another with all wisdom." (Colossians 3:15–16)

12th year—"Let us therefore make every effort to do what leads to peace and to mutual edification." (Romans 14:19)

13th year—"But the wisdom that is from above is first of all pure, then peace-loving, considerate, submissive, full of mercy and good fruit, impartial, and sincere." (James 3:17)

14th year—"Set your minds on things above, not on earthly things." (Colossians 3:2)

15th year—"I will be careful to lead a blameless life . . . I will walk in my house with a blameless heart." (Psalm 101:2)

16th year—"Peacemakers who sow in peace raise a harvest of righteousness." (James 3:18)

17th year—"Blessed is the man who does not walk in the counsel of the wicked, or stand in the way of sinners, or sit in the seat of mockers." (Psalm 1:1–4)

18th year—"Get rid of all bitterness, rage and anger, brawling and slander, along with every form of malice." (Ephesians 4:31)

19th year—"Bear with each other and forgive whatever grievances you may have against one another. Forgive as the Lord forgave you." (Colossians 3:13)

20th year—"But from everlasting to everlasting the Lord's love is with those who fear him, and his righteousness with their children's children—with those who keep his covenant and remember to obey his precepts." (Psalm 103:17–18)

CONCLUSION

Parenting with Eternity in View

A FEW YEARS AGO Boyce and I came in after school to find my bedroom ransacked. Drawers were upside down on the bed. Clothes thrown across the floor. Bathroom cabinets and every inch of my closet had been rummaged through. In the dining room, the pillow shams from my bed were hanging out of the sideboard, as if the intruders had been stopped in their tracks.

The police surmised the thieves were most likely in the house when I had come home unexpectedly at lunch that day, and with nowhere to go, they had waited in the back until I left to go back to work.

Terrifying thought.

Missing were the few pieces of non-costume jewelry I owned, with the exception of a treasured slide bracelet my husband had given me on our fifteenth wedding anniversary. Gone, too, was the "rock" that had been my mother's engagement ring. My wedding set, gone. Antique pins I wore on special occasions, gone. Priceless mementos to me, but worth little to the thieves.

Several neighbors and friends came over after the police arrived. Two friends took me aside for prayer. As they prayed for the return of the stolen pieces, my heart swelled with compassion. The only prayer that would fall out of my mouth was for the souls of the thieves. I prayed that the spirit in their hearts was met by the Spirit in my home and that they would find their way out of a life of crime. I pleaded for mercy.

Little did my friends know that in my heart I was thanking the Lord for His amazing grace for a sinner such as me. Had it not been for His love and mercy, this could have been the life I was leading.

You see, I did something shameful when my twin sons were seven months old. It's a chapter in my life only a very few close friends and my sons have known about. I've kept the secret not out of self-protection, but out of protection for the One I love most dearly, for fear of tarnishing my Christian witness.

I grew up in a Christian home. My mother was, and is, an exemplary woman of faith. Perfect, no, but she loves with a passion untouched by anyone I've ever known. Mother lives to love others. She lives to give.

Daddy meant the world to me, even though he was a grizzly bear—tough, feisty, a man of few words and fewer displays of affection. Underneath his gruff demeanor was a teddy bear's heart, but few ever saw it.

From adolescence to college, if I wasn't at home or school, I was probably at the church. I've loved the Lord since the day I asked Jesus to live in my heart at the age of seven. But the day came when I ignored His voice of warning and failed the test.

My husband and I were leaving the next morning for his job interview. I had taken the boys to stay with my mother while we were out of town and stopped at the discount store to pick up a couple of things. I had admired a soft "leatherlike" belt on a previous trip to the store, but our budget didn't allow for extras.

"You don't need it," whispered a still, small voice.

Ignoring the voice, I took a quick look to see if it was still there. It was hanging in the same spot.

I remember thinking how much I wanted that belt. *I deserve it,* I thought. *It won't be noticed.*

But that still, small voice interrupted my thoughts again, "You don't *need* it."

But I do need *it!* I thought.

"Let me be all you need," whispered the voice to my heart.

The next thing I know, I'm rolling up the belt and putting it in my pocket. I left the store as if nothing out of the ordinary had happened. The security officer approached me from behind and asked me to show her what I had in my pocket. I didn't say a word as I handed the belt to her.

The police were called and I was arrested for shoplifting. I'm not going to use the excuse of postpartum depression. Nor am I going to say it was an accident. I'm not going to blame anyone but myself. You have no idea how many times I've asked myself and the Lord why I did something so utterly wrong, so utterly stupid.

It was a belt—a belt at a discount store. I don't think it cost more than five dollars. I met with an officer of the court for three months and that was the end of it. Or at least for the court that was the end of it. I repented before my heavenly Father and begged for His forgiveness. Tried to figure it out, but couldn't. Tried to put it out of my mind, and succeeded most of the time, but the day thieves ransacked our home, the memory once again became acute.

Boyce, two policemen, and a couple of neighbors were standing in my bedroom as I searched the drawers in the jewelry chest to make a list of missing pieces. Chad's voice broke through the tension, "Mom, Mom, where are you? Mom, Mom!" No one had reached Chad to warn him of what he would find when he arrived home from football practice.

Just as he ran in the room, I lifted the slide bracelet from a drawer in the jewelry chest lying on the bed. I couldn't believe my eyes. Everything else was gone. Everything, but this one, precious keepsake. My sons knew what that bracelet meant to me. We agreed God must have made it invisible to the thieves' eyes. God let us know He was there and had been all along.

A Scripture verse on top of the bureau next to my jewelry chest read, "The Lord is gracious and compassionate, slow to anger and rich in love." The easel was still in place, but the framed verse was turned face-down. I've often wondered if those words were read and felt in the hearts of those who broke into my house that day.

I pray so, because I know what it is to be forgiven. I know what it is to be shown mercy. I know what it is to be humiliated. My greedy, selfish heart might have ruined my life, but God allowed me to be caught the first time I shoplifted, stopping trouble before it even started. I had walked with Him since childhood, He had a plan for my life and as He promises, He will complete the good work that He began in us (see Philippians 1:6), no matter what it takes.

I'm eternally grateful to my parents that even in our less-than-perfect home, the first three names I learned to speak were Momma, Daddy, and Dod. (I had trouble with the "g" sound.) When I was asked to point to "Momma," I pointed to Mother. "Where's Daddy?" I pointed to Daddy. When someone asked, "Where's God?" I pointed all around the room and then to my heart.

My heart breaks as I look around at the kids of today. Those from good homes who fall into drugs, promiscuous sex, and a host of illegal and immoral behavior. Those from troubled homes who run into the arms of gangs to find a "family." Those who can't see a better life because they're buried in poverty. Those who can't see their arrogance because they're blinded by wealth.

The answer for our children is Christ. Did you know that 85 percent of those who come to Christ, come by the age of thirteen?[1] We're born with sinful hearts, capable of rebellion. Our children desperately need us to fill their hearts to overflowing with our love. They also need hearts filled with faith so when those moments of testing come, they'll hear God's voice warning of impending danger, and heed His words.

God was merciful and stepped in to stop me when I failed to listen to His warning. He didn't rescue me, but he stopped me. He used that awful incident to fill my heart with compassion. I know what my heart is capable of on my own. God was with me in that trial, and He will be with your children, too, if they are His.

Our children need us to point them to "Dod."

> Dear Lord, I do not ask that Thou shouldst
> give me some high work of Thine,
> Some noble calling, or some wondrous task.
> Give me a little hand to hold in mine.
> Give me a little child to point the way.
> Over the strange, sweet path that leads to Thee.
> Give me a little voice to reach to pray,
> Give me two shining eyes Thy face to see.
> The only crown I ask, dear Lord, to wear is this,
> That I may teach a little child.
> I do not ask that I may ever stand among
> the wise, the worthy, or the great.
> I only ask that softly hand-in-hand, a child
> and I may enter at the gate.
>
> AUTHOR UNKNOWN [2]

Movies with a Purpose

The goal of family time at the movies is more than entertainment. It is a time to develop relationships and build discernment and character into your kids. Movies can provide a venue for discussions about character traits and values, providing you with opportunities to establish a biblical basis in your children for making choices and understanding worldviews.

Here is a recommended list of movies that can provide enjoyment as well as a provocative and interesting way for your family to discuss morals, values, and character.

Suitable for children under twelve years old, but enjoyable for all ages

Snow White and the Seven Dwarfs (Disney, 1938) animation/family rating = G. An evil queen pursues Snow White, a beautiful princess. Snow White escapes to the forest, where seven adorable dwarfs, who are miners, take her in. Will Snow White escape the evil queen and live happily ever after?

Character traits demonstrated: humility, acceptance of others, kindness.

Family Talk

1. How does Snow White show humility?
2. How is the queen evil? What is bad about her?
3. How do the dwarfs show kindness?

APPENDIX A

Bambi (Disney, 1942) animation/family rating = PG (a scary forest fire; deer's mother dies). Bambi, a young deer growing up in the wild, finds himself alone after the death of his mother. Bambi makes forest friends and learns about the challenges of forest life. When the hunters arrive, Bambi must find the bravery his father possessed to lead the other deer to safety.

Character traits shown: mother/son love, friendship, courage, growing from loss.

Family Talk

1. How do Bambi and the forest animals show friendship?
2. When are times Bambi is brave?
3. Is Bambi's life easy or hard?

Prince of Egypt (DreamWorks, 1998) animation/family rating = PG (some action and scary scenes). Set in ancient Egypt. Moses is a prince who learns he was born a Hebrew slave. He flees Egypt, but returns later as directed by God to free the Hebrew slaves. The Egyptian pharaoh who was once Moses's brother, won't let the people leave until God intervenes.

Character traits shown: choosing good, listening to God, self-sacrifice for greater good, relying on God.

Family Talk

1. Who really saved the Hebrews, Moses or God?
2. How did God and Moses work together?
3. What did Moses give up to do good and obey God?

The Incredibles (Disney, 2004) action/animation rating = PG (some action and violent scenes). A family of superheroes live unknown and quietly in a suburban town. Though they live a simple life, they wish they could be fighting evil again. A top-secret assignment sends them back into action, but it turns out to be not what they expected.

Character traits shown: community service, doing good, courage, value of family love and togetherness.

Family Talk

1. How does the family take care of one another?
2. What do they do when dangerous and evil things happen? Do they run away or look to do good?
3. How does the family laugh and have a sense of humor?

Babe (Universal Pictures, 1995) family fantasy rating = G. Babe, a small pig who is large in personality and character, earns the love of humans and animals alike. Babe meets the challenges of farm life and becomes special friends with one of the sheepdogs, Fly. With Fly's help and Farmer Hoggett's intuition, Babe embarks on a career in sheepherding with some surprising results.

Character traits shown: kindness, determination, humility, cooperation.

Family Talk

1. How does Babe show humility?
2. Which farm animals are uncooperative with the farm owner and the other animals? How and why?
3. Why is Babe so determined and how does he succeed?

Charlotte's Web (Walden Media, 2006) family fantasy rating = G. *Charlotte's Web* is a classic story of loyalty, trust, and sacrifice that comes to life in this live-action adaptation. Dakota Fanning plays Fern, who keeps an unlikely pet—a pig named Wilbur. As winter comes, the family decides that Wilbur would make delicious smoked ham on their dining table. Charlotte, an "ugly" and small spider with a big heart, saves his life with her web and words.

Character traits shown: compassion, humility, friendship.

Family Talk

1. How many God-incidences can you recall from the movie—everyday co-incidences that are not humanly possible?
2. How did Charlotte live out true humility—the ability to put the needs of others ahead of your wants?
3. How did the characters show the love of Christ to others? Wilbur? Charlotte? Fern? Templeton?

For families and children over thirteen years old

Cast Away (DreamWorks, 2000) action rating = PG-13 (action and some disturbing images). Chuck, a Federal Express manager, leaves his true love, Kelly, on Christmas Eve to deliver a package. The plane he is on crashes in the Pacific Ocean, and he is stranded alone on a desert island. He survives on the island alone for over four years. When Chuck is rescued and returns to the United States, his life and goals are completely changed.

Character traits shown: endurance through trials, perseverance, love.

Family Talk

1. How does Chuck endure in trials?
2. Why does Chuck let Kelly go? Does this show sacrificial love?
3. Would you turn to God on a desert island? How would it change life on the island?

Ben-Hur (MGM, 1959) historical epic rating = PG to PG-13 (action, story elements, some disturbing images). *Ben-Hur* is a classic, history-based epic involving issues of loyalty, friendship, revenge, forgiveness, faith, life, and death. The action takes place in Israel during the time of Christ. Ben-Hur and his closest friend, Messala, literally and figuratively struggle with loyalty to one another and to their identities. One of the most discussed parts of the movie is a fierce chariot race between the main characters viewed by a cast of thousands.

Character traits shown: family and cultural loyalty, faith, courage, forgiveness.

Family Talk

1. What causes the conflict between Ben-Hur and Messala?
2. How does Ben-Hur show courage?
3. How does Ben-Hur begin to forgive the things that happen to him and his family?

March of the Penguins (Warner and National Geographic Feature Films, 2005) rating = G. The movie is an entertaining and gripping documentary of penguin life in the Antarctic. It portrays the unique family building that takes place during their migration each year.

Character traits shown: endurance, self-sacrifice, courage.

Family Talk

1. How do the father and mother penguins show self-sacrifice and love for their family?
2. In what specific circumstances do the penguins show courage?
3. In what ways does the life of the penguins speak about our Creator?

Apollo 13 (Universal, 1995) rating = PG. Based on the true story of the ill-fated thirteenth Apollo mission bound for the moon, which took place a year after the first man walked on the moon. When the words, "Houston, we have a problem," came from the spacecraft, everyone knew this would not be a routine mission. The astronauts successfully met many life-threatening challenges with courage and determination.

Character traits shown: heroism, maintaining composure under pressure, overcoming adversity.

Family Talk

1. How do the astronauts relate to one another under pressure?
2. What obstacles do the characters have to deal with? Which are the scariest to you?
3. What prepared the astronauts to survive surprises and circumstances? How do you prepare for similar times?

To Kill a Mockingbird (Universal Pictures, 1962) rating = PG. This classic movie is based on Harper Lee's Pulitzer Prize–winning book of 1960. Atticus Finch, a lawyer and single-parent father in the 1930s, defends a black man and his own family against racial prejudice. Two children watch as their principled father takes a stand against intolerance.

Character traits shown: courage, acceptance, self-sacrifice, family.

Family Talk

1. How did Atticus Finch display courage?
2. What does racial prejudice lead to in a family and society?
3. What family sacrifice and self-sacrifice did Atticus have to make?

It's a Wonderful Life (Hal Roach Studios/Liberty Films, 1946) rating = G. Another classic that should be part of your holiday celebration every year. An angel helps a compassionate businessman who finds himself at the end of his rope. He's given the unique privilege of seeing what life would have been like if he never existed. A film of family values and goodwill based on the life of one man and how his life touches so many other lives.

Character traits shown: loyalty, family love, friendship, dedication, hard work.

Family Talk

1. What is George Bailey's relationship to the town in which he lives?
2. What specific things does George learn about his life and his relationship to others?
3. How does George show loyalty to his friends and family?

A Walk to Remember (Warner, 2002) rating = PG. A troubled, aimless North Carolina teenage boy becomes unexpectedly involved with a minister's daughter. A heartbreaking secret challenges their relationship and those around them.

Character traits shown: endurance, faith, passion for life, personal growth.

Family Talk

1. Describe the teenage girl's passion for life.
2. What role does faith play in the girl facing her secrets and future?
3. In what ways is an openness to change and to other people important in the movie—and in life?

Last of the Mohicans (20th Century Fox, 1992) rating = PG-13 (some violence and frightening images). The movie is the 1992 film adaptation of the classic early American tale by James Fenimore Cooper. An independent American trapper defends innocents caught in the British-French-Indian war in the mid-eighteenth-century frontier.

Character traits shown: bravery, personal loyalty, self-sacrifice.

Family Talk

1. How do Hawkeye and his two Mohican friends show loyalty?
2. How do Hawkeye and his friends show bravery?
3. What bad things come of Magua's obsession for revenge?

The Lord of the Rings (Trilogy, New Line Cinema/MGM, 2001, 2002, 2003) rating = PG-13 (battles; very scary images). An imaginative and stirring movie fantasy on the struggle of good and evil based on the books by J. R. R. Tolkien.

Character traits shown: loyalty, determination, overcoming fear, endurance, bravery, self-sacrifice, resisting evil.

Family Talk

1. How do those in the *Fellowship of the Ring* show loyalty?
2. What sacrifices do the Hobbits undertake?
3. What would have happened had Frodo and the others turned back?

The Simple Life of Noah Dearborn (Lionsgate, 1999) no rating, made-for-TV movie. An inspiring story of an ageless carpenter, Noah Dearborn, who was a master of his craft. He has spent his days working selflessly to take care of others. When a greedy land developer attempts to purchase Dearborn's land and he refuses, there is an attempt to have him declared incompetent. Rather than succeeding, the developer finds Noah's adherence to his simple life too much to overcome.

Character traits shown: value of hard work, perseverance, unwillingness to compromise, beauty of simple living.

Family Talk

1. Who was happiest—Noah or Christian?
2. Name three lessons learned about being an influence in other's lives.
3. Which scene depicted true righteous anger?

The Ultimae Gift (Twentieth Century Fox, 2007) rating = PG. Jason has grown up to become a classic aristobrat, living off a trust fund from his legendary grandfather, Red Stevens. When Red dies, Jason only comes to the funeral to collect "his" millions. What he didn't know was that Red was determined to do after his death what he had been unable to do while living—teach Jason the true value of life. Built into his will are a series of tasks Jason must complete before he can receive a monetary gift from his grandfather's estate. In this process Jason learns the greatest lesson of all—that in order to find his life, he must first lose it.

Character traits shown: personal growth, faith, self-sacrifice, true friendship.

Family Talk

1. What is the impact of Jason's friendship with Emily?
2. Describe the importance of the twelve gifts Jason received from his grandfather.
3. How do Jason's gifts transform his heart? Do you think this will be a lasting transformation?

For families with children sixteen and older

This list has only two movies, both rated R. The themes are so important they are included.

Schindler's List (Universal Pictures, 1993) rating = R (very disturbing themes and images, violence). Oskar Schindler, an Austrian businessman, saves over eleven hundred Jews in World War II by harboring them as workers in his factory.

Character traits shown: courage, self-sacrifice, doing good, recognizing evil.

Family Talk

1. What kind of sacrifices did Schindler make to save others?
2. What would make you take these kinds of risks?
3. What kind of people were involved in the evil in the movie?

*Braveheart (Universal Pictures, 1995) rating = R (violence). Yes, this is a bloody movie, but it is not violent for shock value, but an accurate depiction of a valiant fight for freedom. William Wallace, a thirteenth-century Scottish rebel, an uprising against the cruel English ruler Edward Longshanks, who wishes to seize the crown of Scotland. The Scots are upset about the brutal English invaders, but they lack the leadership to fight back. Wallace becomes their uncompromising leader because of his deep-rooted beliefs that men are entitled to freedom. He courageously stands for his people and inspires

---

*This is my all-time favorite movie. I insisted my sons watch it when they were sixteen. I know of no greater movie displaying faith in God alone, single-minded devotion to the purpose for which God created us, and the beauty and sanctity of the covenant of marriage.

them to defend themselves. The message of this movie is powerful, and life-changing. One man *can* change the fate of an entire country.

Character traits shown: courage, seeking and fulfilling God's will, confidence that strength is found in God alone, ultimate unselfishness.

Family Talk

1. Who was William Wallace willing to die for?
2. Describe the power of one as seen in the movie.
3. How did William Wallace's choices affect the people of Scotland?

APPENDIX B

State Family Policy Councils

(As of August 1, 2007)

Alabama

Alabama Policy Institute
Gary Palmer, President
402 Office Park Dr., Ste. 300
Birmingham, AL 35223
Phone: 205-870-9900
E-mail: garyp@alabamapolicy.org
Website: www.alabamapolicy.org
Fully Associated

Arizona

The Center For Arizona Policy
Cathi Herrod, President
7227 N. 16th St., Ste. 250
Phoenix, AZ 85020
Phone: 602-424-2525
E-mail: info@azpolicy.org
Website: www.azpolicy.org
* Fully Associated *

Arkansas

Family Council
Jerry Cox, President
414 S. Pulaski, Ste. 2
Little Rock, AR 72201
Phone: 501-375-7000
E-mail: info@familycouncil.org
Website: www.familycouncil.org
* Fully Associated *

California

California Family Council
Ron Prentice, Executive Director
P.O. Box 20012
Riverside, CA 92516
Phone: 951-354-8362
E-mail: ronp@californiafamily.org
Website: www.californiafamily.org
* Fully Associated *

Colorado

Colorado Family Institute
Jim Pfaff, President & CEO
P.O. Box 558
Castle Rock, CO 80104
Phone: 877-239-7355
E-mail: info@family.org
Website: www.cofamily.org
* Fully Associated *

Connecticut

Family Institute of Connecticut
Brian Brown, Executive Director
P.O. Box 260210
Hartford, CT 06126
Phone: 860-548-0066
E-mail: info@ctfamily.org
Website: www.ctfamily.org
* Fully Associated *

Florida

Florida Family Policy Council
John Stemberger, President
4853 S. Orange Ave., Ste. C
Orlando, FL 32806
Phone: 407-251-5130
E-mail: JohnS@FLFamily.org
Website: www.FLFamily.org
* Fully Associated *

Georgia

Georgia Family Council
Randy Hicks, President
5550 Triangle Pkwy., Ste. 160
Norcross, GA 30092

Phone: 770-242-0001
E-mail: randy@gafam.org
Website: www.georgiafamily.org
* Fully Associated *

Hawaii

Hawaii Family Forum
Kelly M. Rosati, Executive Director
6301 Pali Highway
Kaneohe, HI 96744-5224
Phone: 808-203-6704
E-mail: info@hawaiifamilyforum
.org
Website: www.hawaiifamilyforum
.org
* Fully Associated *

Idaho

Cornerstone Institute of Idaho
Julie Lynde, Executive Director
P.O. Box 191023
Boise, ID 83719-1023
Phone: 208-863-7804
E-mail: general@
cornerstoneofidaho.org
Website: www.cornerstoneofidaho
.org
* Progressing toward Association *

Indiana

Indiana Family Institute
Curt Smith, President
55 Monument Cir., Ste. 322
Indianapolis, IN 46204
Fax: 317-423-9421

E-mail: ifi@hoosierfamily.org
Website: www.hoosierfamily.org
* Fully Associated *

Iowa
Iowa Family Policy Center
Chuck Hurley, President
1100 N. Hickory, Ste. 105
Pleasant Hill, IA 50327
Phone: 515-263-3495
E-mail: info@ifpc.org
Website: www.iowaprofamily.org
* Fully Associated *

Kentucky
The Family Foundation
Kent Ostrander, Executive Director
P.O. Box 911111
Lexington, KY 40591
Phone: 800-255-5400
E-mail: tffky@mis.net
Website: www.tffky.org
* Fully Associated *

Louisiana
Louisiana Family Forum
Gene Mills, Executive Director
655 Saint Ferdinand St.
Baton Rouge, LA 70802
Phone: 225-344-8533
E-mail: info@lafamilyforum.org
Website: www.lafamilyforum.org
* Fully Associated *

Maine
Christian Civic League of Maine
Michael Heath, Executive Director
P.O. Box 5459
Augusta, ME 04332-5459
Phone: 207-622-7634
E-mail: email@cclmaine.org
Website: www.cclmaine.org
* Fully Associated *

Maryland
Association of Maryland Families
Doug Stiegler, Executive Director
P.O. Box 106
Annapolis, MD 21404
Phone: 410-760-9166
E-mail: director@mdfamilies.org
Website: www.mdfamilies.org
* Progressing toward Association *

Massachusetts
Massachusetts Family Institute
Kris Mineau, President
100 Sylvan Rd., Ste. 625
Woburn, MA 01801
Phone: 781-569-0400
E-mail: mafamily@mafamily.org
Website: www.mafamily.org
* Fully Associated *

Michigan
Michigan Family Forum
Brad Snavely, Executive Director
P.O. Box 15216
Lansing, MI 48901-5216

Phone: 517-374-1171
E-mail: info@michiganfamily.org
Website: www.michiganfamily.org
* Fully Associated *

Minnesota
Minnesota Family Institute
Tom Prichard, President
2855 Anthony Lane S., Ste. 150
Minneapolis, MN 55418-3265
Phone: 612-789-8811
E-mail: tom@mfc.org
Website: www.mfc.org
* Fully Associated *

Mississippi
Mississippi Center for Public Policy
Forest Thigpen, President
P.O. Box 13514
Jackson, MS 39236
Phone: 601-969-1300
E-mail: mail@mspolicy.org
Website: www.mspolicy.org
* Fully Associated *

Montana
Montana Family Foundation
Jeff Laszloffy, President
P.O. Box 485
Laurel, MT 59044
Phone: 406-628-1141
E-mail: jeff@montanafamily.org
Website: www.montanafamily.org
* Fully Associated *

Nebraska
Family First
Dave Bydalek, Executive Director
P.O. Box 82114
Lincoln, NE 68501
Phone: 402-435-3210
E-mail: info@familyfirst.org
Website: www.familyfirst.org
* Fully Associated *

New Hampshire
Cornerstone Policy Research
Karen Testerman, Executive
    Director
136 N. Main St., Ste. 2
Concord, NH 03301
Phone: 603-228-4794
E-mail: cornerstone@nhcornerstone
    .org
Website: www.nhcornerstone.org
* Progressing toward Association *

New Jersey
New Jersey Family Policy Council
Len Deo, President & Executive
    Director
P.O. Box 6011
Parsippany, NJ 07054
Phone: 973-781-1414
E-mail: len@njfpc.org
Website: www.njfpc.org
* Fully Associated *

North Carolina

North Carolina Family Policy Council
Bill Brooks, President
P.O. Box 20607
Raleigh, NC 27619
Phone: 919-807-0800
E-mail: admin@ncfamily.org
Website: www.ncfamily.org
* Fully Associated *

Ohio

Citizens For Community Values
Phil Burress, President & ED
11175 Reading Rd., Ste. 103
Cincinnati, OH 45241-1997
Phone: 513-733-5775
E-mail: info@ccv.org
Website: www.ccv.org
* Fully Associated *

Oklahoma

Oklahoma Family Policy Council
Mike Jestes, Executive Director
3908 N. Peniel Ave.
Bethany Bank Tower, Ste 100
Bethany, OK 73008-3458
Phone: 405-787-7744
E-mail: info@okfamilypc.org
Website: www.okfamilypc.org
* Fully Associated *

Oregon

Stronger Families For Oregon
Mike Howden, Executive Director
P.O. Box 948
Salem, OR 97308
Phone: 503-585-9383
E-mail: michael@oregonfamily.org
Website: www.strongerfamilies.com
* Fully Associated *

Pennsylvania

Pennsylvania Family Institute
Michael Geer, President
23 N. Front St.
Harrisburg, PA 17101
Phone: 717-545-0600
E-mail: mail@pafamily.org
Website: www.pafamily.org
* Fully Associated *

South Carolina

Palmetto Family Council
Oran Smith, President & ED
P.O. Box 11953
Columbia, SC 29211-1953
Phone: 803-733-5600
E-mail: email@palmettofamily.org
Website: www.palmettofamily.org
* Fully Associated *

South Dakota

South Dakota Family Policy Council
Chris Hupke, Executive Director
P.O. Box 88007
Sioux Falls, SD 57109
Phone: 605-335-8100
E-mail: mail@sdfamily.org
Website: www.sdfamily.org
* Fully Associated *

Tennessee

Family Action Council of Tennessee
David Fowler, Executive Director
2479 Murfreesboro Rd. #362
Nashville, TN 37217-3554
Phone: 615-469-4209
E-mail: info@factn.org
Website: www.factn.org
* Fully Associated *

Texas

Free Market Foundation
Mr. Kelly Shackelford, President
903 E. 18th St., Ste. 230
Nathaniel Barret Building
Plano, TX 75074
Phone: 972-423-8889
E-mail: info@freemarket.org
Website: www.freemarket.org
* Fully Associated *

Virginia

Virginia Family Foundation
Victoria Cobb, Director of
  Legislative Affairs
One Capital Square
830 E. Main St., Ste. 1201
Richmond, VA 23219
Phone: 804-343-0010
E-mail: vafamily@familyfoundation
  .org
Website: www.familyfoundation.org
* Fully Associated *

Wisconsin

Family Research Institute of WI
Julaine Appling, Executive Director
P.O. Box 2075
Madison, WI 53701-2075
Phone: 608-256-3228
E-mail: fri@fri-wi.org
Website: www.fri-wi.org
* Fully Associated *

APPENDIX C

Mall Management Companies

After you've talked to the manager of your local mall about the indecent and inappropriate displays in storefronts, find the national company that owns the mall. You would be amazed how much difference a phone call can make from a private citizen. Be bold and courageous.

Feldman Mall Properties, Inc.
2201 E. Camelback Rd., Ste. 350
Phoenix, AZ 85016
Phone: 602-277-5559
Fax: 602-277-7774

1010 Northern Blvd., Ste. 314
Great Neck, NY 11021
Phone: 516-684-1239
Fax: 516-684-1059
E-mail: momentum@feldmanmall
   .com
Website: www.feldmanmall.com

General Growth Properties
110 N. Wacker Dr.
Chicago, IL 60606
Phone: 312-960-5000
Website: www.ggp.com

Simon Property Group, Inc.
225 West Washington St.
Indianapolis, IN 46204
Phone: 317-636-1600
Website: www.simon.com

The Taubman Company
200 E. Long Lake Rd., Ste. 350
Bloomfield Hills, MN 49303-0200
Phone: 248-258-6800
Website: www.taubman.com

The Westfield Group
11th Floor, 11601 Wilshire Blvd.
Los Angeles, CA 90025
Phone: 310-478-4456
Fax: 310-478-1267
E-mail: internet@westfield.com
Website: www.westfield.com

Notes

CHAPTER 1: THE MIRROR OR THE WINDOW?

1. Amy Carmichael, Mountain Breezes: *The Collected Poems of Amy Carmichael* (Washington, PA: CLC Publications, 1999), 149–50. Used by permission.

2. Adapted from the original text of Jacob and Wilhelm Grimm, *Sneewittchen, Kinder-und Hausmärchen* (*Children's and Household Tales—Grimms' Fairy Tales*), final edition (Berlin, 1857), 53.

3. John Mark Ministries, "The Mirror," Found online: jmm.aaa.net.au/articles/17952.htm.

CHAPTER 2: "ENOUGH" IS NEVER ENOUGH

1. U.S. Environmental Protection Agency statistics, accessed online www.epa.gov/epaoswer/osw/.

2. Author unknown, "Toddler Property Laws," April 22, 2002. Found online: www.opt.indiana.edu/clinics/pt_educ/bv_peds/toddler.htm.

3. *Ben Franklin's Almanac of Wit, Wisdom, and Practical Advice* (New York: Bristol Park Books, 2003), 190.

4. Victor Lebow, *The Journal of Retailing*, Spring 1955, 7, as quoted in

Michael Jacobson *Marketing Madness*, 1995, 191. Found online: www.target earth.org/about/conscientious_consuming.html#ref_04.

5. Size of the average new home: U.S. Bureau of the Census, cited by National Association of Home Builders, "Housing Facts, Figures & Trends 2004." Average household size: U.S. Census Bureau, "Average Population per Household and Family: 1940 to Present."

6. "Showcase home" 2004 versus 2005: National Association of Home Builders and The National Council of the Housing Industry, "2005 New American Home" and "2004 New American Home."

7. Materials for new home: National Association of Home Builders, "Housing Facts, Figures & Trends 2004"; NAHB Research Center, "2001 Builders Practices Survey."

8. Size of new homes and cleaning: "Maid to Order: The Politics of Other Women's Work," *Harper's Magazine*, April 2000; "Monster Houses? 'Yes,' " *Planning*, May 2002.

9. Three-car garages: National Association of Home Builders, "What 21st Century Home Buyers Want," in "Housing Facts, Figures & Trends 2004."

10. Solar energy and plumbing: U.S. Census Bureau, "American Community Survey, 2003 Multi-Year Profile."

11. Multiple head showers: On The House with the Carey Brothers, "Tip of the Day: Shower Tower Luxury."

12. Heating oil and hot water: National Oil Heat Research Alliance, "Efficient Oil Heat: An Energy Conservation Guide."

13. Sub-Zero refrigerators: "Trading Up (or Down?)," *Appliance Magazine*, July 2003.

14. Luxury kitchen versus Habitat for Humanity: The Boston Consulting Group, "The New Luxury: Why the Middle Market American Consumer Wants Premium Goods and How Companies Create Them," November 2002; U.S. Habitat for Humanity, "What are Habitat Houses Like in North America?"

15. Borgen Project, World Bank, U.S. Department of Commerce, Census Bureau, Economic Census, 2002.

16. Bill McKibben, "Reversal of Fortune," *MotherJones*, March/April

2007. Found online: www.motherjones.com/news/feature/2007/03/reversal_of_fortune.html.

17. Keisha Lamothe, "Extravagant toys for spoiled rich kids," CNNMoney.com, www.poshtots.com.

18. Ibid., www.mobileation.yahoo.net.

19. Ibid., www.faoschwarz.com.

20. Ibid., www.netkidswear.com.

21. Press Release from New American Dream, "Children's Exposure to Advertising Is Making Them Sick," September 7, 2004. Found online: www.newdream.org/about/BookReleaseFinal.pdf.

22. David Suzuki, "How Much Stuff Is Enough?" July 19, 2002. Found online: www.davidsuzuki.org/About_us/Dr_David_Suzuki/Article_Archives/week1.y07190201.asp.

23. Federal Reserve Statistical Release, "Consumer Credit," April 6, 2007. Found online: www.federalreserve.gov/releases/g19/Current/.

24. "Less can mean more," New American Dream, Found online: www.newdream.org/buy/buyingless.php.

25. Caroline Mayer, "Girls Go from Hello Kitty to Hello Debit Card," *The Washington Post*, October 3, 2004. Section A, 1.

26. Second homes: National Association of Realtors, "Profile of Second Homes: 2004 Update."

27. Statistic box, *Time,* January 1, 2007, 70.

28. Brian Williams, "Enough about You," *Time*, January 1, 2007, 78.

29. DVD, Brad Bird, *The Incredibles* (Walt Disney Pictures, Hollywood, CA, 2004).

30. DVD, Oliver Stone, *Wall Street* (20th Century Fox Productions, Hollywood, CA, 1987).

31. Donna Phillips Munson, "The Catechism for Young Children," *Belonging to Christ* (Lenoir, NC: PLC Publications, 1999), 43.

32. "Readers Write: Are Young People Narcissists?" AlterNet, March 14, 2007. Found online: www.alternet.org/story/49193/.

CHAPTER 3: START WHERE YOU ARE WITH A PARENTING PLAN

1. Max Lucado, *Just Like Jesus* (Nashville: Thomas Nelson, 1998), inside front flap.

2. Lewis Carroll, *Alice in Wonderland*, Barnes & Noble Classics (New York: Fine Creative Media, 2003), 73.

3. *Random House Dictionary of the English Language*, Second Edition (New York: Random House, 1987), s.v. *teenager*.

4. Read the story in 1 Samuel 1–2.

5. Read the story in Luke 1–2.

CHAPTER 4: TAKE CHARGE OF YOUR CHILD

1. AirTran statement reported on WKMG local News 6, Orlando, FL, January 26, 2007. Found online: www.suzatlarge.wordpress.com/2007/01/26/i-will-certainly-fly-airtran-next-chance-i-get-if-theres-room-left/.

2. "A Home May Be Either," *Tony's Scrap Books* (Chicago: Reilly & Lee Co., 1930), 105.

CHAPTER 5: MEET ALL THEIR NEEDS, NOT ALL THEIR WANTS

1. DVD, James Fritzell, Everett Greenbaum, *The Andy Griffith Show,* "Opie and the Spoiled Kid" (New York: CBS Productions, 1963). Used with permission.

2. "Thanks to Ads, Kids Won't Take No, No, No, No, No, For an Answer," New American Dream. Found online: www.newdream.org/kids/poll.php.

3. Sugandha Jain, "Too Much of a Good Thing," *Parent Wise Austin*, December 2006.

4. Connie Dawson, David J. Bredehoft, "The Unwanted and Unintended Long-Term Results of Overindulging Children: Three Types of Overindulgence and Corrective Strategies for Parents and Institutions," *Compelling Perspectives on Counseling* (Washington, D.C.: Walx, G. R., & Yep, R. K., 2005), Article 18.

5. Rev. Harold Wilke, *Sermon Illustrations*, Found online: www.sermon illustrations.com/a-z/p/parenting.htm.

CHAPTER 6: NURTURE GOD-CONFIDENCE

1. Reuters, "Schoolgirl loses 'virginity ring' fight," July 17, 2007. Found online: uk.reuters.com/article/topNews/idUKL1617339420070716?feedType =RSS.

2. Based on a piece by David, "The Foolishness of God," Christian Fellowship Devotionals, March 22, 2000.

3. Dr. Albert Schweitzer, found online: www.sunshin.org/treasure12 .htm.

4. Mark Caro, "It's her party, she'll praise if she wants to" (*Chicago Tribune*, February 20, 2007).

5. Truett Cathy, quote from a speech given at the Retailers' Choice Awards at which the author was present, Atlanta, GA, July 11, 2004.

6. "10 Benefits of Serving Others," *Ideas for Parents*, Search Institute, Newsletter #12, p. 1.

7. John Ruskin, *The Works of John Ruskin* (New York: John Wiley & Sons, 1887), 260.

8. Welland, Colin. *Chariots of Fire*, special ed. DVD. Directed by Hugh Hudson, Burbank, CA: Warner Home Video, Inc, 2005.

9. Ibid.

10. Ibid.

CHAPTER 7: DEVELOP A PASSION FOR COMPASSION

1. National Family Volunteer Awards, "The Barta Family." Found online: www.pointsoflight.org/awards/nfva/winners.cfm#barta.

2. Taken from an interview with Brett Butler on CBS's *20/20* television program, July 18, 1997.

3. Max Lucado, "Receive First, Give Second," Upwards, Inc. Found online: www.maxlucado.com/pdf/upwords.receive.first.pdf.

4. Ellen Iscoe, Ph.E., "5 Steps to Raising a Compassionate Child,"

Washington Parent, May 2007. Found online: www.washingtonparent.com/ articles/0705/compassionate.html.

5. Ibid.

6. James Strong, LL.D., *Strong's Complete Dictionary of Bible Words* (Nashville: Thomas Nelson Publishers, 1996), ref. 5381.

7. Adapted from the following article: Wesley R. Willis, "Full Service Christians in a Self-Serve World," *Discipleship Journal,* Issue #53, Sep./Oct. 1989. Found online: http://www.navpress.com/EPubs/DisplayArticle/1/1.53 .10.html.

CHAPTER 8: BUILD FAMILY TOGETHERNESS

1. "Teens Who Have Frequent Family Dinners Also Likelier to Get Better Grades in School," *The National Center on Addiction and Substance Abuse at Columbia University Report,* September 13, 2005. Found online: www .tvland.com/press/pdf/091305FamilyDinner.pdf.

2. Ibid.

3. Ibid.

4. Kathleen Zelman, "The Family Dinner: Nutrition and Nurturing," April 14, 2005. Found online: www.onhealth.com/script/main/art.asp?article key=56091.

5. George Washington's Thanksgiving Proclamation, 1789. Found online: www.leaderu.com/humanities/washington-thanksgiving.html.

CHAPTER 9: EDUCATE THE HEART IN FORGIVENESS

1. Mamie Gene Cole, "The Child's Appeal," Found online: http://schools .southampton.k12.va.us/education/staff/staff.php?sectionid=237&PHPSES SID=086231a130210241ec4a9c5c253ac9e1.

2. Marti Garlett, *Kids with Character* (Portland, OR: Multnomah Press, 1989), adapted from pages 20–23.

3. Statistics found online: www.childhelp.org/resources/learning: center/ statistics.

NOTES

CHAPTER 10: EDUCATE THE HEART IN GENEROSITY AND GRATITUDE

1. Unknown author, Adaptation of "Perspectives." Found online: www
.inspirationpeak.com/cgi-bin/stories.cgi?record=24.

2. David Staal, "I Thank God For . . . ," Christianity Today International.
Found online: www.christianitytoday.com/childrensministry/articles/ithank
godfor.html.

3. David McCullough, *Truman* (New York: Simon & Schuster, 1992),
55.

CHAPTER 11: GIVING LOVE TO YOUR COMMUNITY

1. Jan Johnson, *Growing Compassionate Kids* (Nashville: Upper Room
Books, 2006), 97–98.

CHAPTER 12: MAKING A DIFFERENCE IN OUR WORLD

1. *The Sourcebook for Teaching Science*. Found online: www.csun.edu/
science/health/docs/tv&health.html.

2. *Top 5 Games in America*, Via Amazon, July 2007. Found online: ds.qj/
net/Top-games-in-America-via-Amazon/pg/49/aid/97087.

3. Million-Minute Family Challenge: History of Board Games. Found
online: www.millionminute.com/history1800.as.

4. Ibid.

5. Theodore Roosevelt, Quote DB. Found online: www.quotedb.com/
quotes/1245.

6. Dwight D. Eisenhower, "An Open Letter to America's Students," *Readings in Freedom* (The Readers Digest Association, Inc.), 43–47. Original article, *The Reader's Digest,* October 1948.

7. Tony Perkins, Louisiana Representative from 1996 to 2004, now the
president of Family Research Council in Washington, D.C.

8. Garth Bardsley, "Michael Moore Pitches 'Sicko' to Teens: 'I'm Telling
You to Stick It to the Man!' " June 28, 2007. Found online: www.mtv.com/
movies/news/articles/1563541/20070627/story.html.

CONCLUSION: PARENTING WITH ETERNITY IN VIEW

1. George Barna, "Evangelism Is Most Effective among Young Kids," Barna Survey, October 11, 2004. Found online: www.barna.org/FlexPage .aspx?Page=BarnaUpdate&BarnaUpdateID=172.

2. Author unknown. Found online: www.sunshin.org/treasure7.htm.

About the Author

Jill Rigby is an accomplished speaker, television and radio personality, family advocate, and founder of Manners of the Heart, a nonprofit organization transforming homes, schools, and communities across the country. Whether equipping parents to raise unselfish children in a self-absorbed world, encouraging the education of the heart in our schools, or training executives in effective communication skills, Jill's definition of manners remains the same—an attitude of the heart that is self-giving, not self-serving. She is the proud mother of twin sons who testify to her contagious passion.